First World War
and Army of Occupation
War Diary
France, Belgium and Germany

15 DIVISION
Headquarters, Branches and Services
General Staff
21 September 1915 - 25 October 1915

WO95/1911/3-4

The Naval & Military Press Ltd
www.nmarchive.com
Published in association with The National Archives

Published by

The Naval & Military Press Ltd

Unit 10 Ridgewood Industrial Park,
Uckfield, East Sussex,
TN22 5QE England
Tel: +44 (0) 1825 749494

www.naval-military-press.com
www.nmarchive.com

This diary has been reprinted in facsimile from the original. Any imperfections are inevitably reproduced and the quality may fall short of modern type and cartographic standards.

© Crown Copyright
Images reproduced by permission of The National Archives, London, England, 2015.

Contents

Document type	Place/Title	Date From	Date To
Heading	WO95/1910-2nd 15 Div HQ Gen Staff & Depts Gen Staff- Apps. July 1915		
Heading	15th Division General Staff Jly-Sep 1915		
Heading	15th Division. Report On The Operations From September 21st To September 30th, Inclusive.		
Miscellaneous	Report On The Operations From September 21st To September 30th, Inclusive.	21/09/1915	21/09/1915
Miscellaneous	Casualties Suffered By The 15th Division For The Period 25th, 26th, and 27th September.	25/09/1915	25/09/1915
Miscellaneous	Headquarters. 15th Division.	02/10/1915	02/10/1915
Miscellaneous	45th Brigade-15th Division. Report On Operations From 21st September to the 30th September, both dates inclusive	01/10/1915	01/10/1915
Miscellaneous	Report of 46th Infantry Brigade on Operations between 21st and 30th September.	21/09/1915	21/09/1915
Miscellaneous	The attached general account of the operations on September 25th and 26th, 1915. is forwarded together with:-	25/09/1915	25/09/1915
Miscellaneous	Operations 25th/26th. Reference Trench Map Sheet 36.c. N.W.		
Miscellaneous	Report by C.H.E. 15th Division on Work performed by R.E. Units 21st to 30th September 1913	21/09/1915	21/09/1915
Miscellaneous	R.E. (2). 15th Division.	02/10/1915	02/10/1915
Miscellaneous	9th Gordons (Pioneers).	01/10/1915	01/10/1915
Miscellaneous	Div. Mounted Troops. Report on Operations September 24th to 28th. 15th Divisional Mounted Troops.	24/10/1915	24/10/1915
Miscellaneous	15th Divisional Cyclist Company. Report on action 25th/26th and 27th September 1915.	25/10/1915	25/10/1915
Miscellaneous	Report from 11th Motor Machine Gun Battery-Operations September 21st to 30th, 1915	21/10/1915	21/10/1915
Diagram etc	Sketch-Not To Scale.		
Miscellaneous	Report on Communications during the fighting at Loos and Hill 70, on 25/9/15 and 26/9/15	25/09/1915	25/09/1915
Diagram etc			
Diagram etc	Arrangements for visual Communication		
Miscellaneous	Report of Operations from 21st to 30th September. Medical Services, 15th Division.	21/09/1915	21/09/1915
Miscellaneous	47th Field Ambulance.		
Heading	WO95/1910-3 15 Div HQ Gen Staff & Depts Aug 1915		
Heading	15th Div. G.S. August. 1915		
War Diary	Gosnay	01/08/1915	03/08/1915
War Diary	Drouvin	03/08/1915	27/08/1915

WO95/1910 — 2d

1st Div HQ Gen Staff & Deptl

Gen Staff - Appx.

July 1915

15TH DIVISION

GENERAL STAFF
JLY - DEC 1915

16th DIVISION.

REPORT ON THE OPERATIONS FROM SEPTEMBER 21st

TO SEPTEMBER 30th, INCLUSIVE.

REPORT ON THE OPERATIONS FROM SEPTEMBER 21st
TO SEPTEMBER 30th, INCLUSIVE.

1. Copies of Operation Orders (the last of which were issued on September 21st) were sent to the Fourth Corps at the time of issue. None of these are therefore attached to this report.

2. Preparations for the attack were completed by the night of September 20th; these included:-

(a) The digging of about 8 miles of new communicating and reserve trenches, the latter provided at intervals with splinter-proof cover.

(b) The construction of deep dug-outs for Advanced Divisional, Divisional Artillery, three Brigades and Divisional R.E. Head-quarters.

(c) The provision and stocking of 7 grenade stores, 4 S.A.A. Stores and 2 R.E. Stores in the forward trenches, and of a central R.E. Stores and S.A.A. Depot in QUALITY STREET.

(d) The placing of 10 water tanks and a large number of barrels and petrol tins in the support trenches, and the improvisation of a large regular water supply at FOSSE 7.

(e) Construction of 28 bridges for the passage of guns and transport through the system of trenches.

(f) The multiplication and safe laying of telephone wires and the provision of visual signal stations.

(g) The construction of Advanced and Divisional dressing and collecting stations at FOSSE 7, QUALITY STREET, LE PHILOSOPHE and MAZINGARBE; and of regimental aid posts and a central evacuation trench.

(h) The laying of a tramway from MAZINGARBE to LE PHILOSOPHE, FOSSE 7 and QUALITY STREET for the conveyance of stores

and

and the evacuation of wounded; and the construction of trucks.

(i) The construction of recesses in the front parapet for the gas cylinders, and the conveyance of 996 cylinders into the trenches.

(j) The laying out of a special Divisional road from VAUDRICOURT to MAZINGARBE for passage of troops.

(k) The exact mapping and labelling of all trenches in the area.

(l) The construction of three Russian saps towards the enemy's front line.

(m) The placing of one day's iron ration for the Division in the CORONS DE FOSSE 7.

The above work, together with other minor preparations, was carried out with unremitting energy by the Divisional R.E. working with the 9th Gordon Highlanders (pioneers). The labour demanded from the infantry was great, and was cheerfully and effectively given.

3. The bombardment commenced on September 21st and continued up to the hour of assault on September 25th; during this period the front trenches were lightly held.

The enemy's reply was weak, increasing slightly on the third and fourth days.

The wire on the enemy's front and support trenches was difficult to observe, but was examined nightly by patrols and proved to be well cut. A demonstration by the Divisional Artillery at 4 p.m. on September 23rd drew weak hostile rifle and machine-gun fire.

Our own wire on the front of our assault was cut in diagonal strips on the night of September 23rd/24th.

The

3.

The preliminary moves of the Division were completed by the evening of September 23rd; and at 4 p.m. on the 24th Advanced Divisional Head-quarters moved to MAZINGARBE (next door to Divisional Artillery Head-quarters), the 2nd echelon moving to NOEUX-LES-MINES.

At 8.5 p.m. on the 24th the message to "carry on" was received from Advanced IVth Corps, and brigades began moving into their forming-up places.

At 11 p.m. information was received that IVth Corps Operation Order No. 35 for the attack held good.

4. The troops of the Division were in their forming-up places by 2 a.m. on the 25th. The whole of the infantry and R.E. of the Division were thus formed up underground on a front of 2,000 yards and a depth of 3,000 yards.

At 3.35 a.m. instructions were received that the hour of zero = 5.50 a.m., and all concerned were informed.

5. At 5.50 a.m. the discharge of gas and smoke commenced; the morning was dull, with slight rain; the wind light and varying from S.S.W. to W. The weather conditions were thus not very favourable for an attack by gas.

At 6.30 a.m. precisely the assault was launched.

6. The casualties from shrapnel and machine-gun fire were heavy on leaving our front trenches, but the assault was not checked. The effect of the gas on the enemy's front line was disappointing; the smoke candles provided an effective curtain for covering the assault.

At 6.50 a.m. our infantry were reported to be through the enemy's support trench; and ten minutes later the third lines of the assaulting columns were reported as crossing the German front trench. The reserve (45th) Bde. had begun to move

forward

forward without difficulty.   The smoke was still very thick, making observation difficult.

By 7.40 a.m. the whole of the assaulting columns of both leading brigades had left our trenches, and the brigade reserves were in our front line preparing to follow.   The leading troops of the 44th Brigade had reported at 7.5 a.m. that they were approaching LOOS.

The 180th (Tunnelling) Co. R.E., less two sections already forward, was now ordered up to LE SAULCHOY PME from VERQUIN.

At 9 a.m. the probability of our left being attacked against PUITS 14 Bis owing to the delay of the 1st Division became apparent; a message was therefore sent to Advanced IVth Corps suggesting that the H.A.R. should bombard the strong points in H.25 and H.31 previously indicated to them.   This was done.

At 9.25 am. a report was received from 73rd Brigade R.F.A. that they had seen our infantry advancing through G.36.b and G.30.d at 9.10 a.m.

8.   At 9.30 a.m. orders were issued through the C.R.E. to prepare crossing places for the cavalry and artillery over our own and the German front line trenches.   This task was allotted to the 74th Field Co. assisted by the 180th Co.   A portion of the latter company had already been placed at the disposal of the Divisional bombing officer for the transport of grenades to the assaulting brigades.

At the same time the C.R.A. was instructed to move up two batteries to positions of readiness at FOSSE 7.

Our infantry were now reported to be in PUITS 14 Bis and advancing up Hill 70.

9.   At

5.

9. At 9.50 a.m. the greater part of the leading brigades were through or past LOOS; and the 45th (reserve) Brigade was in our front line trenches, less one battalion which had moved on in support of the 44th Brigade.

As the advance had gone so fast, the C.R.A. was now instructed to arrange to group the 70th Bde. R.F.A. with the 44th Infantry Brigade and the 71st Bde. R.F.A. with the 45th Infantry Brigade, and brigades were so informed.

This grouping was cancelled again in the evening.

10. At 10.20 a.m. the 1st Division reported that their 2nd Brigade was hung up in front of the German front trench by the wire, and asked that a battalion from the 45th Bde. be detached to work northwards to assist. The great extent of ground now covered by our own troops did not admit of the detachment of a battalion for this purpose. The grenadiers of the 6th Camerons were, however, ordered to bomb northwards and rendered great assistance in relieving the situation.

The 46th Infantry Brigade reported Hill 70 taken at 10.10 a.m. and estimated the casualties of the brigade at 10 per cent.

11. The 45th Infantry Brigade were now ordered to push forward their leading battalions on the right and left into the German front line trenches, but no further.

As a matter of fact the right battalion had already gone forward unknown to the Brigadier.

At the same time the 11th H.M.G. Battery was ordered to QUALITY STREET to come under the O.O.C. 44th Infantry Bde. and to be pushed forward to LOOS at his discretion.

Later on orders were sent for this battery to report to 46th Infantry Brigade. The Battery Commander was unable to

do

6.

do this, but went right forward on his own initiative, and rendered valuable service in assisting to hold the line on HILL 70.

12. At 11 a.m. the G.O.C. 46th Infantry Brigade reported his left in PUITS 14 Bis and his right pushing on to CITE ST. AUGUSTE; he reported his left quite exposed and his No. 5 column (half battalion 12th H.L.I., which connected with the 2nd Bde.) checked in the German front trenches and suffering heavily.

A battalion of the 45th Infantry Brigade (6th Camerons) were immediately ordered forward to his support, directed with their right on PUITS 14 Bis.

At 11.15 a.m. the C.R.A. was instructed to arrange with the H.A.R. to lift their barrages previously arranged to N.1.d, N.2.c, N.2.d, and 1000 yards E. of the German trenches on the west of ST. AUGUSTE, and H.26.d.3.6 to north and east.

General McCracken explained the situation by telephone to the Corps Commander, and earnestly pressed for the forward movement of the Army reserves.

At 11.30 a.m. the Divisional Squadron was moved up to join the cyclist company at HAZINGARBE, and the IVth Corps were informed that only two battalions now remained in hand as Divisional Reserve.

13. At noon there were no signs of the approach of other troops to reinforce the Division. The 44th and 46th Infantry Brigades were reported to be holding Hill 70, but unable to progress against CITE ST. AUGUSTE; The losses amongst the troops who had pushed on over the Hill were heavy; and the left flank was exposed owing to the failure of the 1st Division to advance. The 45th Infantry Brigade (less the battalions already detached) was therefore ordered to push on to LOOS and hold it, and release the troops of the 44th and 46th
Infantry

7.

Infantry Brigades to go forward. The R.A.R. were requested to bombard for a complete period of half an hour the trenches and CITE of ST. AUGUSTE; and at 12.40 p.m. the two companies 9th Gordons (pioneers) in reserve were ordered up to LOOS to put it in a state of defence.

14. At 1.40 p.m. the G.O.C. 21st Division and G.O.C. 62nd Brigade arrived at Divisional Head-quarters. The former did not remain to discuss the situation but wrote some message and immediately left again. At 2 p.m. a message was received from Advanced IVth Corps ordering 21st Division to Advance on LOOS via FOSSE 7 and to place the leading brigade at the disposal of 15th Division.

Soon after 2 p.m. the G.O.C. 62nd Brigade returned and the situation was explained to him by General McCracken. Verbal orders were given him to move his brigade by QUALITY STREET to LOOS; to get into touch with the G.Os.C. 44th and 45th Infantry Brigades; if Hill 70 was lost to retake it; if held, to relieve our troops on it; if situation favoured a further advance on CITE ST. AUGUSTE, to act accordingly in co-operation with 44th and 45th Infantry Brigades. He then left. These orders were then confirmed in writing, and sent after him. He was also provided with some trench maps, which he did not appear to possess. He said nothing about the state of his brigade.

The subsequent movements of this brigade are difficult to follow. The leading battalion was reported as reaching QUALITY STREET at 3.30 p.m., but it seems probably that at least one other battalion went more to the south and arrived at LOOS Cemetery. The Brigadier on his return on the 27th reported that he never got touch with his battalions, though

he

he himself met the O.Os.C. 44th, 45th, and 46th Infantry Bdes. Traces of the doings of his battalions are recorded in the reports of the Brigadiers of this Division, which are attached.

Bde.-Maj. 62nd Bde. appeared at Divisional Head-quarters at about 7.30 p.m., received an account of the situation as far as it was known, and the orders given below in para. 16, was provided with maps, and went off again to find his Brigadier.

15. At 2.30 p.m. 44th Inf. Bde. reported mixed bodies of our troops entrenching on the reverse slope of Hill 70 from H.31.b.6.6 to H.31.a.7.2, and at 3.15 p.m. 44th Inf. Bde. H.Q. moved forward to LOOS.

At 4 p.m. 1st Division reported the capture of the Germans who were holding up the 2nd Brigade; at 4.40 p.m. the 2nd Brigade was reported moving forward, and the anxiety as to our left flank was lessened.

16. At 6 p.m. orders were issued to brigades to consolidate their positions from Hill 70 to PUITS 14 Bis connecting up with 47th Division on the right and 2nd Brigade on the left; 45th Infantry Brigade to relieve 44th Infantry Brigade on slopes of Hill 70, the latter to withdraw behind LOOS into Divisional Reserve; 62nd Brigade to place one battalion at disposal of 46th Infantry Brigade and to hold remainder in support of 45th and 46th Infantry Brigades about PUITS 15. These orders were duly acknowledged by all brigades, but apparently the 62nd Brigade were unable to comply.

17. The situation at the close of the 25th was as follows:- The Crest of Hill 70 and the work on top of it were in German hands. A mixture of the troops of the 44th, 45th and 46th Infantry Brigades were digging themselves in below the crest;

the

the line extended to PUITS 14 Bis, which was still held by us. Major Wace, G.S., went down to LOOS in the afternoon and there met all brigadiers in the course of the evening. He was able to explain the situation and materially assist them. During the night the 44th Infantry Brigade was withdrawn to our own trenches.

The general tendency of the advance had been to the south-east towards the CITE ST. LAURENT, rather than due E. This can only be accounted for by the attraction of the natural features, and by the heavy fire which came from the neighbourhood of the DYNAMITIERE. In many of the reports sent in the CITE ST. AUGUSTE was mentioned in mistake for the CITE ST. LAURENT. This tendency to drift south-east was very marked all through the operations.

18. At 9.7 p.m. orders were received from Advanced IVth Corps that the division was to be prepared to resume the offensive on the 26th and the 2nd Brigade was placed under our orders. This latter provision was revoked two hours later, and the 2nd Brigade ordered to rejoin its own Division west of BOIS CARREE.

General McCracken explained to the Corps Commander on the telephone the state of the division and his doubts as to its fitness to resume the offensive.

19. At 11.30 p.m. a telephone message was received from Advanced IVth Corps that the division assisted by the 62nd Brigade would attack Hill 70 at 9 a.m. on the 26th after one hours intense bombardment.

At 1.45 a.m. on the 26th an order was received confirming this message, and orders were issued for the attack to be carried out by the 45th and 62nd Brigades.

20. At

10.

20. At 12.30 p.m. the enemy delivered a counter-attack on the right battalion of the 45th Infantry Brigade which was repulsed by machine-gun fire.

At about 5.30 a.m. the enemy delivered another and heavier counter-attack from the south-east which was repulsed.

At 8 a.m. the bombardment of Hill 70 commenced and was very accurate. At 9 a.m. the assault was delivered and came under heavy machine-gun fire from the S.E. corner of the DOUBLE CRASSIER, and under the fire of our own artillery.

The assault failed; was renewed, and failed again. The 62nd Brigade in support, it is stated, did not come on. Had they done so, the G.O.C. 45th Infantry Brigade considers that the attack would have succeeded, as the enemy were reported to be evacuating the Redoubt.

A request was sent at 8.35 a.m. to 47th Division to be ready to assist with one battalion. A battalion was told off by the 47th Division for this purpose, but the 141st Brigade failing to get into touch with the 45th Infantry Brigade, this assistance was not forthcoming.

21. At about 10 a.m. the situation began to be critical. The retirement of other troops affected the men of the Division who, being mostly without officers, began to retire. The G.O.C 45th Infantry Brigade, some of whose men were on the hill, greatly distinguished himself by rallying men and taking them back, and in this work he was ably assisted by Capt. Sayer, R.E and other officers. The men of the 18th Division responded at once, and the original line was retained; the men of the 62nd Brigade could not be rallied.

22. The situation remained much the same till noon, when an attack delivered by another brigade on our left (presumably of

21st

21st Division) against the CITE ST. AUGUSTE broke in disorder under shell fire and retired from the field. This increased the difficulty of holding the line on Hill 70, which began to break; and apparently it was about this time that PUITS 14 Bis was lost. The men, however, responded to every effort to reform them, and, with the assistance of some 100 volunteers of his own and the 45th Brigade sent forward by G.O.C. 46th Infantry Brigade, the line was reinforced about 5 p.m. and maintained.

23. At 2.35 p.m. the 6th Cavalry Brigade (less one regt.) was placed at the disposal of the Division and pushed forward into LOOS to hold it at all costs with the remaining troops of the Division still there. The remainder of the 46th and 44th Infantry Brigades with the Divisional Squadron and a platoon of cyclists were ordered to hold the old line of German front trenches between the LENS ROAD REDOUBT and the LOOS ROAD REDOUBT, both inclusive.

At 3.30 p.m. the G.O.C. 6th Cavalry Brigade arrived in LOOS and was placed in command of the troops there. The wireless set and pigeons were handed over to him, and 45th Inf. Bde. H.Q. withdrew to QUALITY STREET. All available officers were sent to LE PHILOSOPHE to collect stragglers, and take them forward to our old front trenches. Several hundreds of men of the 21st Division were collected in this way.

At 6.30 p.m. owing to reports received chiefly from the 46th Infantry Brigade that our troops were still holding on to the line on Hill 70, orders were sent to G.O.C. 6th Cavalry Brigade to get into touch with them and reinforce them. Arrangements were made at the same time for the establishment of a barrage of artillery fire to cover them. This barrage was very effective.

24. At

24. At 10.30 p.m. orders were received from Advanced IVth Corps for the 82nd Brigade to rejoin its Division. The remnants of it were therefore collected and sent away.

At 12.25 am. on the 27th orders were issued, in accordance with instructions from Advanced IVth Corps, for the withdrawal of the Division (less artillery) to MAZINGARBE. This was carried out without incident.

At 3.45 p.m. orders were issued for the move of the Division on the 28th to DROUVIN - HOUCHIN - MAILLICOURT.

At 11.30 p.m. the mounted troops were warned to be ready to move at an hour's notice - apparently forward - Nothing happened and the order was subsequently cancelled.

On the 28th the Division moved to the area allotted - one-third of the infantry bivouacked in the open - Headqrs. moved to DROUVIN.

On the 29th Headqrs. moved to LABUISSIERE.

On the 30th one brigade at MAILLICOURT was ordered to move out to make room for the French; it marched to LABUISSIERE and BRUAY.

25. Reports of my Infantry Brigadiers, C.R.E., O.C. Signal Co., O.C. 9th Gordons (pioneers), Divisional Squadron, Cyclist Co., M.K.G. Battery Commanders, and A.D.M.S. are attached. I consider these reports too valuable to be omitted and they are too detailed for inclusion in my own report.

The Divisional Artillery worked throughout under the orders of the IVth Corps, and will doubtless render their report direct. Brig.-Gen. Alexander worked in the closest co-operation with me throughout the operations and rendered valuable service.

The

13.

The work done by the artillery in cutting the wire during the preliminary bombardment, in supporting the attacks, and in placing barrages of fire where required was conspicuously good. The First Group H.A.R. also rendered prompt and effective assistance whenever called upon.

26. I consider that none of my elaborate preliminary preparations were wasted. The division was launched to the attack under the most favourable conditions, the casualties up to the time of the actual assault were negligible, the supply of grenades, ammunition and tools was well maintained, and the large numbers of wounded were attended to and evacuated with despatch.

27. Communications throughout were very good. Except for very short intervals, communication between Division and Brigade Headquarters was maintained by telegraph and telephone during the whole period under report. The wireless and pigeon service proved very valuable in keeping up communication with LOOS. The work of the Divisional Signal Co. was excellent; it was owing to their efforts, and to the frequent reports sent in by artillery observers, and by the officers actually engaged, that I was kept in close and constant touch with the situation.

28. Between 14,000 and 15,000 grenades were taken into action on the men. These proved very useful and materially assisted the advance. The grenadiers of all battalions showed conspicuous courage and resource.

29. The Lewis machine-gun proved a serviceable weapon. The machine-gun detachments greatly distinguished themselves

and

and their losses were heavy. The 11th M.M.G. Battery also rendered most valuable service.

30. I am of opinion that the arrangements for discharging the gas require more organization and study. A number of cylinders remained undischarged, and a good deal of gas found its way into our own trenches.

I suggest that the cylinders should be connected up in batteries, and manipulated from well under cover; also the discharge pipes should be buried in the parapet to prevent their being blown back into the trench by shells.

The smoke candles were very effective. But a holder on a long stick is required for them, so that the candlemen can keep well under cover.

The discharge of gas drew a heavy artillery fire on our front trenches.

31. I have no hesitation in saying that had fresh troops of good quality been held in readiness to follow closely on the heels of my Division, the German line would have been pierced. My Division carried out its orders to the letter, at great speed, and exhausted itself in the effort. The Division sent to support me came too late, and was not in a condition fit to enter such a fight. Its Commander and Staff appeared quite unfamiliar with the ground or the situation and made no effort to get into close touch with me or my Staff. No member of the Staff of the Guards Division or of the XIth Corps came near my Headquarters, though the G.O.C. 3rd Cavalry Division kept in constant touch with me.

It is beyond my province to suggest that the task allotted to the Divisions or Corps destined to support my attack required as careful preparation and previous study

as

15.

as did the task of my Division. But I must beg permission to point out that these precautions were apparently lacking, and to deplore the result.

My orders to push on to the full extent of the power of the Division were clear and definite and were carried out to the full in the confident assurance that the promised flow of reinforcements behind me would be maintained. In the event, I consider that nothing but the high soldierly qualities displayed by officers and men of my Division averted a disastrous retreat from the positions won.

32. I cannot close this report without paying a tribute to the discipline, bravery and resource shown by all ranks under my command.

The spirit of officers and men remains high in spite of the heavy losses sustained, and the fighting value of the division will be completely restored as soon as reinforcements of personnel and material are received.

The following appendices are attached:-

App. 1.	Total Casualties.
,, 2.	Report - O.O.C. 44th Bde.
,, 3.	,, ,, 45th Bde.
,, 4.	,, ,, 46th Bde.
,, 5.	,, of C.R.E.
,, 6.	,, of O.C. 9th Gordons.
,, 7.	,, O.C. Divl. Squadron.
,, 8.	,, of O.C. Cyclist Co.
,, 9.	,, of H.M.G. Battery.
,, 10.	,, of O.C. Signal Co.
,, 11.	,, of A.D.M.S.

8th Oct. 1915.

(Sd) F.W.N. McCracken, Maj.Gen.,
Comdg. 15th (Scottish) Division.

CASUALTIES SUFFERED BY THE 15th DIVISION FOR THE PERIOD 25th, 26th, and 27th SEPTEMBER.

Units.	OFFICERS.					OTHER RANKS.				
	Killed.	Wounded.	Missing.	Gassed.	Total	Killed.	Wounded.	Missing.	Gassed.	Total
H.Q. 44th Bde.	--	--	1	--	1	--	--	--	--	--
9th Black Watch.	8	11	1	--	20	68	314	292	5	679
9th Seaforth Hrs.	5	10	4	--	19	44	362	294	--	700
10th Gordon Hrs.	--	5	2	--	7	23	221	130	--	374
7th Cameron Hrs.	4	6	4	--	14	64	255	215	--	534
13th Royal Scots.	6	9	1	--	16	37	224	105	4	370
7th R.S. Fus.	6	11	1	--	18	63	240	83	--	386
11th A & S Hrs.	7	4	1	--	12	36	214	64	--	314
6th Cameron Hrs.	8	8	--	1	17	30	270	70	--	370
7th K.O.S.Bs.	9	7	3	--	19	12	221	404	--	646
8th K.O.S.Bs.	3	7	4	--	14	23	124	228	4	379
10th Sco. Rifles.	12	5	4	--	21	68	318	239	--	625
12th H.L.I.	7	11	--	--	18	50	184	315	--	588
9th Gordon Hrs. (Pioneers).	5	4	--	--	9	21	179	64	4	268
70th Bde.R.F.A.	--	2	--	--	2	1	12	--	--	13
71st ,, ,,	--	--	--	--	--	1	14	2	2	19
72nd ,, ,,	--	1	--	--	1	--	1	--	--	1
73rd ,, ,,	--	--	--	--	--	2	8	--	--	10
11th M.M.G.Batt.	--	2	--	--	2	--	3	--	--	3
15th Divl.Cyclists.	--	--	--	--	--	1	6	--	--	7
73rd Fd.Co.R.E.	2	2	1	--	5	10	14	29	--	53
74th ,, ,,	--	--	--	--	--	3	3	1	10	17
91st ,, ,,	--	--	1	--	1	9	32	11	--	52
45th Fd.Amb.RAMC.	--	--	--	--	--	--	4	--	--	4
46th ,, ,,	--	1	--	--	1	--	1	--	4	5
47th ,, ,,	--	--	--	--	--	--	3	--	--	3
Totals.	82	106	28	1	217	575	3227	2546	41	6389
Attached Units.										
120 Co. R.E.	--	--	--	--	--	1	22	2	--	25
187 ,, ,,	--	--	--	--	--	--	1	--	4	5

1.   44th Brigade.

Headquarters,
     15th Division.

I have the honour, in accordance with your G.209 of 1-10-15 to report as follows:-

On 21st September, 1915, a bombardment of the enemy's trenches commenced. At that time my Brigade was disposed as follows:-

In X.1 front system	= 10th Gordon Highlanders
In GRENAY-VERMELLES main line trenches	= 8th Seaforth Highlanders.
In billets and dug-outs MAZINGARBE	= 9th Black Watch.
In billets in VERQUIN	= 7th Cameron Highlanders.

The bombardment continued from 21st to 24th instant.

On 22nd September. The 7th Camerons moved from VERQUIN about 7 p.m. and occupied the GRENAY - VERMELLES branch line of trenches.

The casualties during this period were:-

10th Gordon Highlanders	O.R.	10 killed 33 wounded
8th Seaforth Highrs		1 "
7th Cameron Highrs.		3 "
	TOTAL	10 killed 37 wounded

2.   On the night of the 24th/25th September the Brigade moved into position in the forward trench lines for assault.

At 4 p.m. on the 24th the Brigade Headquarters moved from MAZINGARBE CHATEAU to Advanced Brigade Report Centre in QUALITY STREET.

3.   At 2 a.m. 25th September, reports from all units were received that they were successfully in position for the assault.

These included reports from the 73rd Field Co. R.E. and "G" Co. 9th Gordon Highlanders (Pioneers), who were attached to the Brigade.

Night was fine - wind slightly west of south.

4.   Hour of zero was reported at 5-50 a.m.

At 5-50 a.m. gas and smoke discharge commenced. Wind not very favourable and too light causing inconvenience to occupants of front trench.

5.   At 6-30 a.m. the assault was launched - the Brigade moving as follows:-

In two columns each on a front of two platoons:-
The 9th Black Watch on the right, with right flank on the LENS road.
The 8th Seaforths on the left, with flank resting on Boyau 8c.
The 7th Cameron Highlanders were in support.
The 10th Gordon Highlanders were in Brigade Reserve.

I sent one section R.E. and one platoon 9th Gordon Highlanders in rear of each of the assaulting columns.

The 7th Camerons were ordered to support at such a distance as would ensure their being able to reinforce when and where required.

The 10th Gordon Highlanders in Brigade Reserve were ordered as soon as the assaulting columns and supports were clear of the German first line trenches to occupy them, and with the assistance of the two remaining sections R.E. and 2 Platoons 9th Gordon Highlanders (Pioneers) to open up communication trenches from our front line to the German front line and await orders.

At the moment of assault two Companies of the 10th Gordon Highlanders occupied our front line trenches from Sap 18 to the LENS road together with their 4 machine guns and the four machine guns of the 9th Gordon Highlanders (Pioneers), 2 of which were to be in Sap 18 so as to bring an enfilade fire on the LENS ROAD REDOUBT.

All the other machine guns moved with their battalions under orders of the Commanding Officers.

The guns of the 9th and 10th Gordon Highlanders were under the Brigade Machine Gun Officer.

6./

5.

6.   The assault was well carried out, the leading battalions going with great dash over the parapet at the enemy's trenches. The Lens Road Redoubt was strongly held by machine guns, and the casualties were heavy at first, especially in the Black Watch who faced the redoubt.

The defence was quickly worn down and at 7-10 a.m. the columns were reported as over the German 2nd line trench.

7.   At 7-45 a.m. I received a report that the 8th Seaforths were approaching LOOS which they could see through smoke and mist.

The German third line gave little resistance, but some wire in front had to be cut, which caused a momentary delay and a few casualties, as machine gun fire was opened from some houses N.W. of LOOS about G.29.d.1.2.

8.   At 8-5 a.m. the advanced part of the Brigade was reported as in the outskirts of LOOS, the Seaforths on the north and the Black Watch towards the south.

A regular street-to-street and house-to-house fight then took place. Bombing parties doing excellent work in houses and cellars, but the enemy did not make any regular stand as they were kept well on the run and the bayonet was freely used. Some very gallant actions were reported of bombers, who attacked any house from which fire was opened.

A number of Germans surrendered. They seem to have been taken entirely by surprise, as they mostly had no equipment on and everything was left in confusion.

By this time the units had got considerably mixed and the 7th Camerons had mostly joined with the other two battalions.

9.   At about 7-45 a.m. I ordered the 10th Gordon Highrs in Brigade Reserve to move from the German trenches and support the main attack of the ~~44th~~ Brigade leaving it to the Commanding Officer to use his discretion as to where he could best assist in the attack, but at the same time to watch
the right flank

the right flank in case of any counter attack from the direction of LENS.

10. At 8-45 a.m. a report was received from the Black Watch and Camerons that the advanced troops had passed through LOOS. The enemy was still on the run and offering little opposition.

11. At 9-25 a.m. a message received from the O.C. 10th Gordons that he was pushing on with the whole battalion through LOOS as the Camerons were still ahead.

12. From reports received, HILL 70 was occupied, without serious opposition, by the 44th Brigade about 8-30 a.m. as a report sent off at 8-55 a.m. by O.C. 7th Camerons, states machine guns of 9th Gordons had gone up to the Hill with those of the 10th Gordons.

No official confirmation of the HILL was however received until later, when it came from two or three sources.

13. During the fighting through LOOS there was a tendency for the left of the attack to swing round towards the south, pivoting on the right flank. This was partly due to the conformation of the ground, but principally I think from a natural tendency to follow prominent features such as the PYLONS at LOOS and the CRASSIER, so that by the time the Brigade reached HILL 70 the front line was facing nearly S.E.

14. Reports were received about that time that the front of the attack was being held up by heavy rifle and machine gun fire from CITE ST.AUGUSTE, but on comparing this on the map with the Officers who sent reports, there appears no doubt that it should have read CITE ST.LAURENT and the salient at the Dynamitiere which was full of machine guns.

This fire forced those who had proceeded over the hill to retire as it was found impossible to advance in the face of such opposition, and the casualties were numerous, and

eventually

eventually a position was taken up with the CRASSIER as the right about G.36.d.3.5. running through a natural bank about H.31.c.6.9. to H.31.b.2.7.

The German work at H.31.central was not occupied by the enemy on the arrival of the 1st line.

15. All the battalions of the Brigades were now mixed up about 10 a.m. and also some 7th Royal Scots Fusiliers and some of the 46th Brigade. Colonel Sandilands who was on this part of the hill took over command of all the mixed parties near him and commenced digging in and consolidating the position.

It was unfortunate that through over-keenness a number of the Brigade pushed on so far over HILL 70, as it caused a great many casualties who could not be got back.

16. Two reports, one sent at 10-5 a.m. and one evidently later but without hour from Captain G.S.Tuke were received by me at 11-25 a.m. stating his position on HILL 70. This Officer was Brigade Machine Gun Officer and had gone forward with the 8 guns of the Brigade Reserve, viz:- Four each of 9th and 10th Gordons.

I received no further report from him and I regret that he is still missing and I can get no account of where he was seen last.

17. At 10-15 a.m. I ordered my Brigade Signal Officer to go forward and establish communication with LOOS, so that I might advance my Headquarters. He had already carried his line forward to the German trenches.

This he proceeded to do, but I could not get into communication with him, as it appeared afterwards his line was continually cut.

18. At 10-40 a.m. I received a message from 15th Division that the M.M.G.Battery had been ordered to report at my Head-
quarters/

Headquarters, they arrived shortly afterwards and I gave the Officer Commanding instructions to proceed to the N outskirts of LOOS and assist the forward line. This he did, and the battery afterwards did extremely good work at HILL 70, and suffered severe casualties.

19. At 11-10 a.m. I received messages that reinforcements were required, which I sent on to the Division.

I believe the 45th Brigade were then either on their way to reinforce or moved directly afterwards.

Ammunition was also asked for, and as much as possible was sent forward, and I have received no report that at any time the supply failed.

At 1.30 p.m. four machine gun limbers (one per battn) with pack saddles and ammunition, under Lieut Holmes, 8th Seaforth Highlanders, were sent forward to LOOS or as far as they could get and to do what was possible in getting S.A.A. up to the Hill

I also ordered the Brigade tool carts to be horsed and sent forward as soon as it was safe to do so, as the men had very few tools beyond the entrenching tools they carried.

Owing to great congestion of traffic on the LENS road they did not get down until past midnight.

20. At 3 p.m. I moved to LOOS with my Brigade Major and most of the Staff as I had established communication through, leaving my Staff Captain at QUALITY STREET until I arrived.

On arrival in LOOS however I found the wires had been constantly cut and a place under the PYLONS at first chosen was being heavily shelled, so moved to a house near at G.35.b.2.2. where I found the O.C. 7th Royal Scots Fusiliers. He was endeavouring to establish telephone communication but his lines were constantly out of order.

Communication was consequently to a great extent lost and only kept up to a limited extent by runners from units to QUALITY STREET.

21.

21.   At about 5 p.m. a battalion of East Yorkshire Regt. arrived belonging to the 62nd Brigade which I had been told was coming up to relieve my brigade. I met the commanding officer who asked me the way to Hill 70 and I showed him, pointing out to him which side of the PYLONS to keep. He informed me the remaining battalions of the 62nd Brigade were also just arriving.

He then went forward but apparently joined with the 142nd Brigade on our right.

I saw no other troops of the 62nd Brigade and I tried to find the Brigadier as I was told he was in LOOS, but could not get hold of him.

22.   About 7.45 p.m. Colonel Sandilands 7th Camerons and Captain Strange 8th Seaforths came to my temporary Headquarters and discussed the situation with Major Wace representing 15th Division.

It was decided to place Colonel McClear 13th Royal Scots in command of the troops on the hill and for him to see how much he could relieve the remains of my brigade.

Colonel McClear then left with Colonel Sandilands and my Brigade Major, Major Rainsford Hannay for Hill 70.

23.   I remained until my Brigade Major reported to me that Colonel McClear had consolidated the position and had arranged for the Seaforths and Camerons to be relieved at once and that they were proceeding on their way back into reserve.

Major Hannay remained until the other two battalions were relieved and then rejoined me in QUALITY STREET.

Brig-Gen. F.E.Wallerstein, Commanding the 45th Infantry Brigade had arrived at the same Headquarters during the time these arrangements were being carried out and I left him there on my return.

24. On my way back I found troops lining some of the German third line trenches and was told that they were another Yorkshire battalion of the 62nd Brigade. I did not see any Northumberland Fusiliers. On arriving at the main LENS Road I found it terribly congested with transport, mostly 1st line cookers, etc., it was impossible to move carts anywhere. The next morning a lot of it was destroyed as well as animals by the enemy's shells.

I don't know how it got there.

I had only ordered my Brigade tool carts and some water carts to go down under cover of darkness and to return before daylight. My tool carts were handed over to the 45th Brigade, but it was impossible to get them back. I have since sent for them but though most of the tools were there on the 28th the wagons were smashed.

25. By 6 a.m. 26th September what remained of my Brigade were back in the GRENAY - VERMELLES line of trenches.

I then got an order to move them to our original front line trenches and later they were ordered to the German trenches which they occupied at dusk and were established there when I went round later in the evening and were in touch with the 8th K.O.S.Bs on their left.

26. During the day a great many stragglers belonging to various regiments were returning along the LENS Road towards QUALITY STREET in rather disorder.

I got some officers of my brigade and 45th Brigade and some police and stopped as many as we could.

I collected various officers and put them in charge and eventually sent about 400 to man the front British trenches North of the LENS Road.

/They

They consisted of Yorkshire Regiments, Northumberland Fusiliers (2 Battalions), Somerset Light Infantry and others.

Later I got a large number of Lincoln Regiment and Durham Light Infantry and odd lots, placed them under officers and sent them to the front line British trenches S. of the LENS Road when my own Brigade moved into the German trenches.

There were several members of some Divisional Staff arrived during that day but they did not take any steps to collect the men.

The Brigadier and Brigade Major of the 62nd Brigade were at my Headquarters in QUALITY STREET during part of the day.

27. About 1.30 a.m. 27th September an order was received for the 44th Brigade to move into billets at MAZINGARBE.

This order was carried out and they arrived in MAZINGARBE between 3 a.m. and 5 a.m. and went into billets under arrangements made by the Staff Captain.

I went with my Headquarters for that night to Chateau ARNAUD but moved in the morning later to MAZINGARBE CHATEAU.

I attach a list of casualties as far as can be made out.

Since the 27th September several parties of men have turned up.

One party of one N.C.O. and 10 men of 9th Black Watch had got detached from their battalion when going through LOOS on 25th September and joined a battalion of the 47th Division on our right. They remained with this battalion under a Captain Williams until the afternoon of the 28th when they returned when relieved, staying that night at LES BREBIS
 ing
AND REPORT/HERE the next day.

28.   In conclusion I should like to speak of the splendid behaviour of all ranks.   Though a stream of wounded were returning all day on the 25th there were no sound men returning with them.

The slightly wounded cases were helping those who could not get on by themselves. The very large proportion were making their own way, even badly wounded cases. One man of the Camerons was wounded in the hand with another wound in the head, he had on his back a comrade who was shot through the leg.

All were cheery - no grumbling or complaining.

Many after their wounds were dressed went by foot into NOEUX LES MINES rather than take up room in ambulances which were required for more severe cases. Several after being dressed both officers and men returned to the firing line and remained until relieved.

Where all did so well it would be invidious to make distinctions and it is difficult to say which had the most right to be proudest, the officers of their men, or the men of their officers.

The young officers proved themselves most devoted to their duties, sticking to their work after being wounded.

The 73rd Field Coy. R.E., and "C" Coy 9th Gordon Highlanders must be included in the excellent work of the Brigade.

Both suffered heavy casualties in officers and men.

List of recommendations for good service has been forwarded separately.

In the Field.
2nd Oct., 1915.

(sd) M.C.WILKINSON. Brig-Gen.,
Commanding 44th Infantry Brigade.

46th Brigade - 15th Division.

Report on Operations from 21st September to the
30th September, both dates inclusive.

21-9-15. 13th Royal Scots)
          11th A & S Hrs.) in billets at NOEUX LES MINES.
          Bde Hd. Qrs.   )
          7th R.Scots Fus.) in billets at LABUISSIERE.
          6th Cameron Hrs.)

22-9-15. As above.

23-9-15. 3 p.m. Bde Headquarters moved to NOEUX LES MINES.

          5.30 p.m. 6th Camerons moved to billets and bivouac at
          DROUVIN.

          9.30 p.m. 7th R.Scots Fus. moved to billets and bivouac at
          VAUDRICOURT.

24-9-15. 8.30 p.m. Bde Headquarters moved to advanced Headquarters in
          LENS Road Redoubt.
          Battalions of the Brigade marched to MAZINGARBE into
          positions of readiness.

25-9-15. The Brigade complete was in position of readiness at 1.30 a.m.
          cookers and water carts were with their battalions until
          shortly before dawn when they rejoined the remainder of the
          1st Line Transport at the walled in triangle south of
          MAZINGARBE CHATEAU; the horses of these cookers and water
          carts only remaining with their vehicles. All other
          animals being sent to NOEUX LES MINES.
          At 5.50 a.m. a 40 minutes discharge of gas interspersed with
          smoke from candles was delivered after which the assault by
          the 44th and 46th Infantry Brigades was launched punctually
          at 6.30 a.m. The 46th Infantry Brigade in touch with the
          two leading Brigades, commenced moving forward until 9.30 a.
          m. when it occupied the positions in our front line system
          of trenches, two battalions in each of the areas occupied
          by the 44th and 46th Infantry Brigades respectively. Owing
          to the receipt of an order, said to have been passed from
          the Brigade reserve of the 46th Infantry Brigade on their
          left, the 7th R.Scots Fusrs (less their battalion Headquarter

                                                              followed /

followed the 44th Infantry Brigade through LOOS to HILL 70, where they are reported to have materially assisted in the retention of the western slope of the hill.

At 10.10 a.m. the grenadiers of the 8th Camerons were put under the orders of the G.O.C. 46th Infantry Brigade and proceeded to bomb northwards along the German front line trench from SOUTHERN GAP towards LOOS TRIA in order to assist the 2nd Infantry Brigade held up opposite that front. This bombing party progressed for 60 or 70 yards but were stopped by a strong barrier manned by hostile bombers with a machine gun.

At 11.30 a.m. the 5th Camerons, under orders received from the 15th Division, were sent forward with their right directed on PUITS 14 bis to support the left of the 46th Infantry Brigade and with orders to place themselves under the command of the G.O.C. 46th Infantry Brigade.

At the same time the 7th R.Scots Fus. were ordered to move forward into the German third line trenches between LOOS Cemetery and G.29.c.5.9 when it was discovered that they had already moved forward. They were at once sent an order not to proceed further forward than HILL 70 and were to place themselves under the orders of the G.O.C. 46th Infantry Brigade. The 11th A & S Hrs being ordered, instead, to man the German third line trench west of LOOS.

At 11.40 a.m. the 12th R.Scots were sent forward to hold the German front line trench from LENS Road Redoubt to LOOS Road Redoubt.

At 12.10 p.m. the 12th R.Scots and 11th A & S Hrs were ordered forward into LOOS and to hold it in order it release troops of the 44th and 46th Infantry Brigades and to be ready to reinforce either of those Brigades, if called upon by them to do so. At this hour Brigade H.Q. moved forward to QUALITY STREET and there found 44th Infantry

Brigade /

Brigade Headquarters.

At 5.10 p.m. news was received that the 62nd Infantry Bde. had been ordered to move on LOOS, and, if HILL 70 was still held by our troops, to, if necessary, relieve them.

At 5.30 p.m. the leading battalion of the 62nd Brigade passed through QUALITY STREET.

News from the 13th R.Scots and 11th A.& S. Hrs now became scarce and nothing definite was discovered until Major Wace, G.S. 15th Division arrived from LOOS and explained the situation.

The 13th R.Scots and 3 companies of the 11th A. & S.H. had been called upon to support the leading brigades on HILL 70 and the 45th Infantry Brigade was now to relieve such parts of 44th and 46th Infantry Brigades as the situation would admit. Major Wace had seen Lt.Col.McClear, D.S.O. 13th R. Scots and placed 3 companies of 13th R.Scots, 7th R.Scots Fusiliers and 3 companies 11th A.&.S.H. under him with orders that he was to consolidate the position.

At 8 p.m. Brigade Headquarters moved forward to LOOS and relieved the G.O.C. 44th Infantry Brigade. It was ascertained that the troops on HILL 70 were much mixed up but owing to the situation a re-grouping was not possible. Tools were got forward and ammunition and the companies proceeded to improve the trenches they had already dug with what available tools they had carried and with their entrenching implements. The enemy's artillery was active throughout the evening and night, their fire being directed on the troops holding the slope of HILL 70, upon LOOS village and upon the LENS Road.

26-9-15. At 12.30 a.m. the enemy delivered a counter attack on the 7th R.Scots Fus:, the right hand battalion of the Brigade. The attack was easily repulsed our machine guns being greatly aided by a large fire from the enemy's rear in the direction of LENS which showed up the attackers very distinctly.

At 5 a.m. /

-4-

At 5 a.m. orders were received to attack in conjunction with the 62nd Infantry Brigade the REDOUBT on the North East end of HILL 70 and to occupy the hill, to cover an attack by 21st and 24th Divisions.

The battalions being much scattered the task of organising them for the attack was difficult in addition to which the enemy delivered, at about 5.30 a.m., a heavy counter attack from a South-easterly direction.

The G.O.C. 62nd Inf. Bde. and O.C. Battns were consulted and the attack was arranged to take place at 9 a.m., after an hours intense bombardment by all available guns.

7th R.Scots Fus. on the right, 11th A. & S.H. in the centre, 13th R.Scots on the left closely supported by three battalions of the 62nd Infantry Brigade.

As the right hand battalion was to keep touch with the 47th Division throughout and it was feared this battalion would be drawn in towards the REDOUBT thereby causing a gap, assistance was asked for and a battalion of the 47th Infantry Brigade was ordered to cooperate and cover the right flank of the attack.

The forward troops, ordered to be drawn back to a safe distance during the bombardment could not be withdrawn before 8 a.m., for fear that the enemy might advance and occupy the trenches left vacant, but were successfully retired a short distance immediately the guns opened.

The bombardment was extremely accurate in spite of the difficulties to observation caused by a mist, though a certain number of shells fell on our front line.

At 9 a.m. punctually whistles were blown and the front line went forward.

The enemy's fire was heavy, particularly that which enfiladed the Hill from the direction of the S.E. corner of the DOUBLE CROSSIER. The left and centre of the assaulting line came under our own artillery fire and the attack failed, though

supports/

supports were brought forward and another charge was
attempted.

The supporting brigade, it is stated, never came on, though
had it done so it seems extremely probable that the position
would have been carried. One officer, since killed, who
succeeded in reaching the outer defences of the REDOUBT,
stated that he saw the defenders running away back.

At 11.10 a.m. two battalions, which have not yet been clearly
identified retired hurriedly from the neighbourhood of PUITS
14 Bis leaving our left flank exposed. One of these
battalions was however rallied and once more took up its
position in the line. During this time the Brigade was
shelled and was under rifle and machine gun fire all of which
caused heavy casualties.

Reinforcements were asked for and it was pointed out that
with their left flank exposed the battalions would find
difficulty in maintaining their position.

A message was received that reinforcements were arriving.
One battalion to LOOS and another battalion from NORTH MAROC-
both of the 47th Division - but these battalions were not
seen.

At 12 noon a fresh Brigade commenced an attack against the
enemy's trenches in front of CITE ST AUGUSTE but never
developed and failed to progress.

On being heavily shelled the attack completely collapsed and
with no apparent signs of any attempts to rally, the troops
returned rapidly to the German 1st Line trenches. The
failure of this attack and arrival of reports that the
Germans were advancing as if to outflank our left made the
position appear most precarious, reinforcements were asked
for and it was pointed out that unless the recent attack
was reformed the Brigade would be unable to retain its
position.

Parts of the line held by the brigade now began to suffer

further /

further losses and to fall back until a message was received that they were now holding the lower slopes of HILL 70. on the outskirts of LOOS, where they were told to hold on. Ammunition supply became difficult over the open, men were not available to carry it up from the Brigade Reserve and sufficient men to carry it could not be withdrawn from the firing line.

At 1.5 p.m. an order was issued to battalions that if forced to retire they were to do so on the German front line trenches between LOOS ROAD and LENS ROAD REDOUBTS. The line on the western slopes of HILL 70 was held until between 4 and 4.30 p.m. when through some mis-interpretation of the above order those portions of regiments that could be collected were withdrawn to LOOS just at the time that the village was entered by the 6th Cavalry Brigade. Parts of the Brigade remained under the orders of the G.O.C. 6th Cav.Bde and assisted in holding the village until late that night when they were relieved and withdrew to the VERMELLES BRANCH of the GRENAY Line.

Throughout the 25th and 26th the intercommunication between battalions and the Bde. and between the Bde. and the Division was remarkable. At times the wires from LOOS to QUALITY ST. were cut but messages were got through by both carrier pigeons and short range wireless - the latter however being "jammed" after the third message had been sent.

27-9-15.	The brigade was billeted in MAZINGARBE.
28-9-15.	The brigade marched to billets in HAILLICOURT.
29-9-15.	The brigade marched to LABUISSIERE, halted for the day and in the afternoon 3 battalions moved to billets in BRUAY.
30-9-15.	The 3 battalions at BRUAY returned to LABUISSIERE and bivouaced.

Sd. F.G.WALLERSTEIN. Br.General.
1-10-15. Commanding 46th Infantry Brigade.

REPORT of 46th INFANTRY BRIGADE on OPERATIONS between
21st and 30th September.

September 21st.

1. On September 21st the Artillery commenced their first day's bombardment; confining their attention principally to efforts to cut the German wire entanglements, their shooting was very accurate and considerable damage was done to the German wire and also to the LOOS ROAD REDOUBT. There was practically no retaliation on the enemy's part.

The situation of the Brigade this day was as follows:-

7th Bn K.O.Sco.Bord.	PHILOSOPHE & MAZINGARBE.
8th Bn K.O.Sco.Bord.	LABEUVRIERE.
10th Bn Scottish Rifles.	MAZINGARBE.
12th Bn High. L.I.	Occupying the front system of trenches in Sector X.2 and part of X.1 with Headquarters at QUALITY STREET.

The wind caused considerable anxiety by remaining in the East, and officers in the front system were detailed to take meteorological observations at 4., 4.30 and 5 a.m. each day.

September 22nd.

2. The bombardment continued throughout the night and during this day.

The practice made by the Gunners still remained excellent and by this evening the wire was practically sufficiently cut to enable an attack to succeed. No effort was made to cut the wire on the North side of LOOS ROAD Redoubt. There was still but little effort to reply on the part of the German artillery. During the night of 21st/22nd, and, in fact, during each night of the bombardment, heavy rifle and machine gun fire was maintained on the German lines to prevent working parties mending their wire.

/Situation

Situation of Brigade:-

7th Bn K.O.Sco. Bord.	All in PHILOSOPHE.
8th Bn K.O.Sco. Bord.	Half Battn MAZINGARBE.
	- do - SAILLY line of defences.
10th Bn Scottish Rifles.	MAZINGARBE.
12th Bn. High. L. I.	Holding front system.

Patrols were sent out to examine the wire and reported that there was a certain amount of low wire which required cutting.

September 23rd. S. Third day of bombardment. Artillery still continued directing its attention to German wire to make certain of it being efficiently cut. It also, of course, fired on the enemy trenches.

At 3.55 p.m. an intense bombardment of the enemy trenches took place, lasting for five minutes. At the end of this time the infantry opened rapid fire and also machine gun fire. Then the Artillery again fired on the hostile trenches. The object was to make the Germans believe an attack was going to take place and so get them to man their trenches when it was hoped the resumption of Artillery fire would kill some of them. They only, however, replied with a few rifle shots but a good many shells were fired into our lines, four men being wounded.

Situation this night:-

7th Bn K.O.Sco. Bord.	One company in front system of trench, 3 companies - PHILOSOPHE.
8th Bn K.O.Sco. Bord.	As on 22nd.
10th Bn Scottish Rifles.	One company in front system of trench, 3 companies in MAZINGARBE.
12th Bn High. L.I.	One company in MAZINGARBE. " " " PHILOSOPHE. Two companies in front system.

/Patrols

Patrols again went out. Those in front of right Company reported wire sufficiently cut - those in front of left companies could not get near enough to see on account of hostile fire.

Our own wire was cut to allow passage of troops.

24th September. 4. Bombardment of hostile trenches and wire continued. Especially vigorous during night 24th/25th to prevent enemy mending wire.

Whole brigade moved into forming up area. The day being cloudy this movement commenced about 4.30 p.m., the whole movement was completed by 11 p.m.

By this hour 11 p.m., every battalion was in its area and arrangements made for giving the men breakfast before starting next morning.

Brigade Headquarters moved to LOOS ROAD KEEP.

25th September.
26th September. 5. See separate report.

27th September. 6. During night 26th/27th the remnants of the brigade moved to MAZINGARBE, it reached here early in the morning and went into billets there.

Throughout the day efforts were made to collect stragglers, and clean up the men. In the afternoon burial parties were sent out.

28th September. 7. Brigade marched to billets at HAILLICOURT. Every effort being made to replace lost kit and equipment.

29th September. 8. Brigade remained in same billets which are insufficient for its needs. During day reinforcements of some 200 men altogether for Brigade arrived.

Classes of working machine gun commenced.

30th September. 9. Brigade received orders to evacuate all billets South of BARLIN - LABUISSIERE Road. This necessitated one battalion bivouacing.

Steady drill and rifle exercises by all battalions.

The attached general account of the operations on
September 25th and 26th, 1915., is
forwarded together with:-

A. Report from 10th Bn. Scottish Rifles, as to action of No.3 Column.

B. Report from 7th Bn K.O.Scottish Borderers, as to the action of No.4 Column.

C. Report from Colonel PURVIS as to the action of No.5 Column. Owing to all the officers of this column having become casualties, this report is not complete.

D. Report from Lt. Colonel PURVIS, 12th Bn. H.L.I. showing the part played by the 12th Bn H.L.I. (less two companies).

E. Report from Lt. Col. SELLAR, 8th Bn. K.O.Scottish Borderers, as to action of reserve.

F. Report from Major POLLARD-LOWSLEY as to the part played by 91st Field Company and "H" Company 9th Gordons.

G. Report from Capt. SAYER, R.E., showing the events of Hill 70 on the morning of 26th September.

K. Further report from O.C., 91st Field Company R.E., (manuscript).

OPERATIONS 25th/26th.

Reference trench map Sheet 36.c. N.W.

1. The morning of September 25th, 1915, broke dull and cloudy with a very gentle wind blowing from between S.S.W. and S.W. At about 5.15 a.m. the wind, from the same direction, increased in strength, but only slightly. Inwardly everyone was wondering whether the wind was sufficiently strong, and from the right quarters, to justify the discharge of gas. At 5.50 a.m., however, these misgivings were quietened, though not actually dispelled, by seeing the discharge commencing. Everyone was then asking "Is it going in the right direction?" There was evident relief when it was seen to be doing so – but slowly, the wind was hardly favourable for this discharge.

From the Brigade Headquarters at LOOS ROAD KEEP the sight of the gas and smoke clouds as they rolled towards the German lines was magnificient; but everything beyond this white and yellow cloud was invisible. A few moments after the discharge began, heavy rifle fire commenced to be poured into our trenches. The German shell fire, however, was not so severe as was anticipated. It was distinctly noticeable how the hostile rifle fire gradually decreased in volume as the fumes reached the German lines; its intensity, however, was only diminished; it never ceased altogether. At 6.15 a.m. the 18th Bn. H.L.I. reported one gas cylinder had burst and that two were leaking badly.

2. Immediately previous to the commencement of the assault Piper LAIDLAW, 7th Bn. K.O.Scottish Borderers, jumped up on to our front parapet and piped away, though gas fumes surrounded him, and heavy rifle fire was sweeping our trenches.

Exactly at 6.30 a.m. the troops crossed the parapet and made for the German lines. As a matter of fact they would have suffered less if they had waited another five minutes or so owing to the slowness with which the gas was travelling; the

/order

order, however, was 6.30 a.m. and so the troops left at that hour; but a considerable number were gassed.

The German wire was crossed without much difficulty, the Artillery having cut it thoroughly. Heavy casualties, however, were suffered between our lines and the German trenches, which shows that the gas was not so efficient as supposed. In fact from what could be seen, and from what others state, it seems to have done more harm to our own troops than to the enemy.

3. No.6 Column suffered heavy losses in crossing into the German trenches, these losses were due:-

(a) To the supposed "Southern Sap" proving to be no sap at all; hence the bombers told off to bomb along it were severely handled. The fact that no sap existed is interesting because the aeroplane photographs distinctly showed a trench there - in reality it was a mere scrape in the ground.

(b) The 2nd Infantry Brigade on our left, not getting on as quickly as was anticipated and so this column suffered severely from rifle fire from their left.

4. By 7.5 a.m. the whole of Nos 3 and 4 Columns had reached the German front system and immediately pushed on. The whole of No.5 Column (less two platoons) were also across by this hour. From this moment the advance was continued steadily by Nos 3 and 4 Columns without much opposition, except shell fire past LOOS, entry into which seemed to be easily avoided by the attacking troops, in spite of several machine guns enfilading our line as they advanced. This, however, may be accounted for by the rapid progress made by the 44th Infantry Brigade through this village.

5. The 2nd Infantry Brigade on our left is stated to have suffered severely from the effects of gas and also to have found the German wire uncut. This resulted in it being completely stopped, and not until well into the afternoon could it get forward and then only, it is understood, by the assistance of another Brigade which was sent to attack these

/German

German trenches from the North east.

Meanwhile our attack progressed rapidly far more so than evidently had been anticipated; but owing to the situation of the 2nd Brigade, the safety of our left flank caused great anxiety. It was on this account also that the situation of No.5 Column was rendered the more difficult. This Column had large casualties on reaching the German front trenches, especially amongst bombers on account of no trench being found in the Southern Sap, and, therefore, it had not the men available to bomb towards the 1st Division. It could only maintain itself in the trenches won with difficulty, losing nine out of ten officers killed and wounded, and more than half its men. Captain Torrance, however, managed to hold on until assistance was sent him in the shape of some 100 bombers of the 6th Cameron Highlanders, and, in addition, one platoon of the same regiment as a covering party.

6. The exposure of our flank had an appreciable effect on the operations. Our troops knowing that the 2nd Brigade should be on their left were continually sending out patrols to look for it. When no trace of it could be found messages were sent back to the Division asking for troops to be sent up at once to protect our left. This resulted in the 6th Camerons being sent up with their right directed on PUITS No.14 Bis. Not only did the rapidity of the attack lead to the exposure of our left flank, but also it placed in serious jeopardy the whole of the assaulting column since no provision had been made to pour in the continual flow of reinforcements so necessary for the success of such an operation. After some time, the remainder of the 45th Infantry Brigade was sent on but this was like a mere drop in the ocean and would have been better if another Division could have been following up close at hand ready to push through the leading Division when that one was exhausted.

The attack started at 6.30 a.m. and instead of a fresh Division being ready to advance at - say 10 a.m., as should

/have

have been the case for a successful termination to the operations, no sign of its arrival was seen until nightfall. If, therefore, the whole of the 45th Infantry Brigade had been pushed in at 10 a.m. there would have been no support for the Divisional Commander to fall back upon in case of a reverse, for some 8 - 10 hours.

7. Our assaulting columns reached the line Hill 70 - PUITS 14 Bis Chalk Pit at about 9 a.m. after suffering considerably whilst getting into the German front line. So easily was Hill 70 captured, however, and so much were the Germans on the run, that the attacking troops could not unfortunately be stopped. This led to their undoing. South of the Hill 70 are the houses belonging to the outskirts of LENS. These had all been placed in a state of defence. They bristled with M.G's and, in addition the Germans rushed M.G's up to the Railway embankment just North of the houses. The troops, exhausted as they were by their vigorous attack and without artillery support, could not face it, and had to withdraw to Hill 70 where they were ordered to consolidate. Here for the remainder of the day attack and counter-attack for its possession continued. It was during this withdrawal that the Brigade suffered heavy casualties.

8. About one hour before dusk, General Matheson went forward with the object of seeing the position at PUITS 14 Bis, but on approaching Chalk Pit Wood he saw the PUITS being heavily shelled so changed direction on to the Chalk Pit. As he did this he met Colonel SELLAR, 8th Bn. K.O.Scottish Borderers who explained the situation on the left to him. General Matheson then went on to Chalk Pit where he met G.O.C. 2nd Brigade and arranged details for night defence, i.e., that 2nd Brigade would be responsible for PUITS No. 14 Bis inclusive.

9. At the end of the day the crest of Hill 70 and the work on top of it was in the hands of the Germans.

/Our

Our troops were digging themselves in just below the crest. The troops holding this line were a mixture of 44th, 45th and 46th Infantry Brigades. Later on in the night the 44th Infantry Brigade was withdrawn. The line held at nightfall was from just below the crest of Hill 70, with a portion of the work in our hands, to PUITS 14 Bis, at which point we were in touch with the 2nd Brigade. Our troops in the work on Hill 70 as well as those below the crest were heavily shelled by our own artillery. At about 7 p.m. General Matheson visited O.O.C. 44th Infantry Brigade in LOOS and met their Major Wace G.S., 15th Division. The Brigade Advanced Headquarters were in a German trench at G.29.b.5.2. Communication with the Division from here was impossible, all four wires which had been laid out being cut. Afterwards it was discovered they were cut by our own troops who had orders to cut all lines in the German trenches. At about 9 p.m., therefore, General Matheson decided to go back to his Headquarters at LOOS ROAD KEEP, where he was better able to get touch with the Division and get out the necessary orders. He left a representative at his Advanced Headquarters. By this time it had been raining heavily for several hours, and all the telephone instruments had got thoroughly soaked rendering them useless. During the night orders were received that PUITS No. 14 Bis would be taken over by the 21st and 24th Divisions, who were responsible for the line from here to the North, while the 46th Infantry Brigade was told it would be relieved by one battalion of the 62nd Infantry Brigade.

10. No communication was received from Headquarters, 62nd Infantry Brigade, as to which battalion was to come under Brigadier-General Matheson's orders. Even the position of the 62nd Brigade Headquarters was not discovered for some time. This was eventually discovered through the 15th Division, and a copy of the order for the battalion which was to relieve the troops of the 46th Infantry Brigade was sent to the 62nd Infantry Brigade Headquarters.

/The

The latter sent this copy on to the Battalion - 13th Northumberland Fusiliers - and the latter received it some time during the night; but there is nothing to show they received some amendments and additions to this order issued later.

Meanwhile during the night Lt. Col. Purvis, Commanding 12th Bn. H.L.I., who had come to Advanced Brigade Headquarters to see General Matheson, and who had been told that a battalion of the 62nd Infantry Brigade would relieve the troops of the 46th Infantry Brigade, found that battalion wandering about looking for 46th Infantry Brigade Advanced Headquarters. Knowing the orders, Lt. Col. Purvis took charge of this battalion, and himself placed it in the position it was to get into during the night. Having done this, Colonel Purvis returned to Brigade Headquarters at LOOS ROAD KEEP and reported his action.

11. At 9 a.m. the 62nd Infantry Brigade was to have attacked Hill 70, the 46th Infantry Brigade remaining in support. This attack was to be preceded by one hour's intense bombardment.

Between 7.30 and 8 a.m. on 26th, General Matheson arrived at his Advanced Headquarters. On arrival, parties of men of the 46th Infantry Brigade were seen coming back from Hill 70. These parties were stopped and ~~asked~~ asked where they were going, they replied that they had been relieved and were told to go back. By this time most of the officers had become casualties, and none was to be seen with these retiring parties. General Matheson, therefore, went forward to the bottom of Hill 70 and stopped all men coming back, placing them in position along the LOOS - BENIFONTAINE Road.

Captain Sayer, 91st Field Company, R.E., was then sent up to stop any more men coming back and place them in the same place, and, generally, to take charge of them. From this position they were well placed to support the attack of 62nd Infantry Brigade on Hill 70.

12. This attack commenced at 9 a.m. and at first seemed to go

/without

without a hitch. Troops poured up Hill 70 and over the crest to the South-west of the work. Most of the work itself was still held by the Germans, but our bombers started working their way through it. The attack between Hill 70 and PUITS 14 Bis did not progress to the same extent, it appeared to suffer considerably from machine gun fire from the direction of PUITS 14 Bis and the Chateau South of it. An attack made between the Chalk Pit Wood and PUITS 14 was stopped by machine gun fire which seemed to come from a red house between this wood and the PUITS. To the North of Chalk Pit Wood, British troops were seen to be wandering aimlessly about, first going forward, then coming back again, going forward a little way and eventually running away. Almost at the same time the troops, who had crossed Hill 70, were seen retiring, some stopped for a few minutes where the remnants of the 45th and 46th Infantry Brigades were digging themselves in just below the crest; but others still kept retiring and eventually the whole, except a very small portion of these 21st Divisional Troops, were in retirement. The handful of men of the 15th Division on Hill 70 rallied the troops of the 21st Division several times but at last the latter were incapable of being rallied any more and went, leaving the remnants of 15th Division with a few remaining men of 62nd Infantry Brigade to hold Hill 70 alone.

13. Beyond a couple of German counter-attacks which were repulsed, there was no reason, apparently, for the panic produced in the 21st Divisional Troops. Certainly the Germans were using asphyxiating shells all that morning, and their artillery fire increased in intensity as if reinforcements of artillery had been received, but beyond this there seemed no cause for panic, except possibly from the fear engendered by machine gun fire. An unrestricted view of the whole front from Hill 70 to Chalk Pit Wood could be obtained from Brigade Advanced Headquarters, and watching this front most carefully through powerful glasses, no sign, except possibly for some dozen men on the

/skyline

skyline, could be seen of any Germans. Nevertheless, the whole battle front was covered with line upon line of men withdrawing. These lines came down Hill 70, swept up past Advanced Brigade Headquarters, back over the original German trenches, over our former/system, and on towards PHILOSOPHE.
front

Many attempts were made by General Matheson and other officers to check this tide, but all in vain, with the exception of a few men of the 15th Division who somehow had got mixed up in it and who at once obeyed the orders given to them. No attempt was made by any ~~other~~ of these troops to stand.

The men seemed incapable of grasping what was said. Ordered to get into trenches and reform, the men merely stared vacantly into one's face and walked on. They appeared bereft of comprehension and yet not a sign of a German was seen.

Realising the situation, General Matheson, about 10.30 a.m. sent a Staff Officer to report to Divisional Headquarters. About 11.30 a.m. as the flow still continued without check, General Matheson, himself, went back to LOOS ROAD KEEP to report the circumstances personally over the telephone to the Division. The Divisional Commander ordered him to Headquarters to report verbally; arriving there about 12.30 he received the G.O.C's instructions to get into touch with the G.O.C. 44th Infantry Brigade and with the remnants of the two brigades, and any men of 21st Division it was found possible to stop, to hold our original front line trenches. Meanwhile two cavalry regiments had been sent up into LOOS to hold that village and support the 15th Divisional troops still on Hill 70.

Arriving at QUALITY STREET, the Brigadiers 44th and 46th Infantry Brigades conferred and decided to hold the original frontage of their respective attacks, i.e., the 46th Infantry Brigade from 8 (c) inclusive to the North.

Leaving QUALITY STREET, General Matheson then went to ~~arrange~~

/arrange

arrange for this occupation, and still met men streaming back. A few of them he managed to stop and got them into our front line trenches. These trenches were full of gas fumes, so the men were allowed to lie down outside. Having organised the defence of this system, General Matheson then went over the German front line trenches where he met the remnants of Capt Terrance's party 12th Bn. H.L.I., with some 6th Cameron Highlanders.

He asked for volunteers to go and assist the remnants of the Brigade on Hill 70, and the whole of this party at once volunteered and went. This was the party that arrived on Hill 70 as the remnants were retiring from it about 6 p.m., and whose arrival helped our men to get back on to the Hill. Still there was no sign of any Germans except their shells, and still the flow of men to the rear continued.

14. In the meantime arrangements were made for feeding and watering our men, and as many of the 21st Division as possible. The one cry of the latter troops seemed to be that they were hungry and thirsty. Our own men, of course, were naturally hungry and thirsty also. Arrangements had been made on the afternoon of the 25th to get the cookers of each battalion to QUALITY STREET in the hope that it might have been possible to get some food to the firing line. Beyond some of the H.L.I., however, it does not seem that any of our other battalions got food. The cookers, however, were in continual use from the moment of their arrival making hot water for the wounded and feeding various stragglers who came in. Their presence helped the situation on the afternoon of 26th and enabled food to be sent up at once to the men holding our front trenches. It was not long, therefore, before all these men were fed. Water was also obtained for these men, there was some difficulty in obtaining it on account of the supply in QUALITY STREET running dry, but it was obtained from LENS ROAD REDOUBT, and carried up to the men in petrol tins.

15.   About 6 p.m. the order came that a Cavalry Brigade was going to hold North LOOS Avenue where it would get into touch with the 1st Division until the arrival of the Guards Division; the 15th Division was to hold the German front system. On receipt of this order our troops, with a number of 21st Divisional Troops, were taken forward and placed in position in the German trenches, the 46th Infantry Brigade and 44th Infantry Brigade dividing the frontage between LOOS Road and the Southern Salient between them.

The Guards Division came up about 7 p.m. and prolonged the line to our left, the Scots Guards being next to the 46th Infantry Brigade and the Irish Guards immediately North of them. In the meantime the O.C. Somerset Yeomanry came in and asked for orders. He was told that presumably he and his dismounted men were to connect along North LOOS Avenue between LOOS and 1st Division, but that he was not under our orders in any way. He tried to telephone to the Cavalry Division but without much success. In the middle of the night he took his men away but ~~away~~ where to is unknown.

Orders were received about 12 midnight to withdraw all men of 15th Division under cover of darkness to MAZINGARBE where they would reform, leaving the Cavalry and Guards to hold the position won. Brigadier-General Campbell, commanding Cavalry in Loos, being responsible for withdrawing the 15th Divisional remnants on Hill 70.

16.   The remnants of the 15th Division had continued to hold their position on Hill 70 throughout the 26th September, repulsing several counter-attacks on the part of the Germans and rallying time after time the withdrawing troops of 21st Division. This remnant had suffered severely from the fire of men of the 21st Division who at one time were in positions behind them. About 5 p.m. they seemed to have withdrawn from the Hill on an order given by some one in the 45th Infantry Brigade; but at

/the

the bottom of the Hill they met some more troops coming up,
100 men, a mixed force of H.L.I. and Cameron Highlanders who
General Matheson had sent forward.

On meeting these men the whole then returned to their
original position on the Hill and remained there until relieved
by the 3rd Cavalry Brigade about 12 m.n. 26th instant.

On relief, the remnant of the Brigade marched back to
MAZINGARBE where they spent the night of 27th and collected
their stragglers, etc.

17. The battle on 25th had not long been in progress before
the problem of ammunition supply arose. Thanks, however, to
the provision of Depots made beforehand, there was never any
actual shortage of ammunition, but there was considerable
difficulty in obtaining men, in requisite numbers, to carry the
ammunition from QUALITY STREET to the Depots in the trenches and
from these up to the firing line.

But the difficulty as regards getting ammunition from
QUALITY STREET to the Depots in the trenches was overcome by
getting up the pack ponies and carrying it on these. The
parties organised in the first instance for getting ammunition
from the trench depots to the firing line was soon used up, and
as the battalion progressed it took a long time for the men to
get from the depots to the firing line and back. However, by
collecting all available men, the supply was kept up somehow,
as, however, there seemed danger of the troops on Hill 70
running short of ammunition, messages were sent ordering up the
S.A.A. carts and these were sent forward to LOOS. They suffered
a number of casualties from shell fire, chiefly, however, amongst
the animals. The troops in the 46th Infantry Brigade seemed to
have been kept well supplied with ammunition, and therefore
little use was made of these carts by them; but the presence of
these carts was justified by the use made of them by the 44th

/and

and 46th Brigades and some troops of 21st Division. The total casualties from sending these forward was 20 animals killed, 14 wounded as well as two carts broken up.

18. The arrangements made for collecting the wounded left much to be desired. The regimental aid posts were established in our front trenches. Advanced Dressing Stations were in QUALITY STREET. The regimental stretcher bearers collected wounded and took them to the regimental aid posts, from here the stretcher bearers took them on to the advanced dressing station. On arrival at the latter, if the case was serious the man was left on the stretcher for fear of hurting him if moved. This resulted, in a short while, in no stretchers being available for the bearers and this led to many of the wounded being left out and it is feared led to the death of many of them.

20. No mention is made here of the many gallant acts that were performed both by officers and men which helped so materially to gain the success achieved. It is presumed that these will all be recorded in the historical records of the Battalions.

This brief summary of the operations cannot however be closed without some slight testimony to the extraordinary fighting spirit displayed by all ranks. Every single officer and man was doing his utmost and nothing would have stopped them getting through. This is a fact well worth recording when it is remembered that about one year ago the profession of arms was foreign to most of these men.

Nothing could have surpassed the dash and fury with which the 12th Bn H.L.I., 7th Bn. K.O.Scottish Borderers, and 10th Bn. Scottish Rifles captured the German front system of trenches.

Report by C.R.E. 15th Division on Work performed by
R.E.Units 21st to 30th September 1915.

Preparatory Work.
1. All the important work in the preparation of our trenches to enable an assault to be delivered from them had been completed before the 21st September, and the special stores collected and prepared by the R.E. for the Infantry Brigades had been issued.

21st to 23rd September.
2. The 73rd and 91st Coys R.E. were employed under the 44th and 45th Inf.Bdes respectively in adding finishing touches to trenches and providing additional splinter proof protection in the forming up trenches.

Advanced dressing stations and first aid posts were completed by these units during this period.

The 74th Coy was concentrated at NOEUX LES MINES and employed on the completion of road diversions and the provision of extra water supplies for R.A. horses in their advanced positions.

24th Sept.
3. During the evening of this day the 74th Coy moved to LE GAULCHOY FARM, MAZINGARBE with one section at the advanced R.E.Store at QUALITY STREET.

The 73rd and 91st Coys moved up to their forming up places preparatory to assault under Brigade orders.

The 180th (Tunnelling) Coy (less one section) came under the orders of the C.R.E. and were located :- H.Q. and one section at LE GAULCHOY FARM, MAZINGARBE, remainder with mechanical and horse transport at L.14.a.9.9 in readiness to move up at short notice when required.

The C.R.E. moved his H.Q. to LE GAULCHOY FARM.

25th Sept.
4.
(a) The 73rd and 91st Coys took part in the assault under Brigade orders.

Half of each company accompanied the assaulting columns of their respective Brigades (one section to each column) the other half of each company moved with the Brigade supports. Parties from each company were detailed to lay

out /

out and superintend the digging of communication trenches from our front line to the German front line trenches.

(b) The two leading sections of the 73rd company reached the ridge of HILL 70 with the leading infantry, both the officers and a large proportion of other ranks had become casualties before reaching LOOS. These two sections remained on the crest of HILL 70 until driven back to a line below the crest where they assisted the infantry to entrench. They were withdrawn about 10 p.m. by order of the G.O.C. 44th Infantry Brigade, but a part of No.2 Section remained behind all night and helped to hold the line.

(c) The remaining half company remained behind the Brigade supports until these advanced. While waiting some trenches over the LENS road were bridged, and while employed on this work one officer and ten men were killed and wounded. This half company followed the 18th Gordons to LOOS and proceeded to HILL 70, the crest of which was reached about 9.30 a.m. Finding some infantry in the Keep hard pressed they advanced to it and endeavoured to hold it. All were driven out and retired behind the crest line began to dig in.

(d) A party of ten R.E. only under Capt Cardew, again advanced and managed to enter the keep but were driven out. They then assisted the infantry to entrench on the slopes of HILL 70 until withdrawn during the night. About 10 men remained all night assisting to hold the line.

(e) Of the leading sections of the 91st Company one (No.3) lost its officer at the commencement of the assault. After assisting infantry to turn the German support trench they proceeded to HILL 70. A barn at G.36.b.8.7 was placed in a state of defence. This section was subsequently combined with No.4, the other leading section which had advanced too far to the left towards that portion of the German trenches which was still held by them. This section suffered heavy losses, and, being unable to advance was ordered to withdraw.

They /

-3-

They were extricated by their officer who displayed the greatest gallantry in rescuing all his wounded under very heavy fire.

(f) The remainder of the Company did good work in the neighbourhood of HILL 70 and PUITS 14 Bis, assisting infantry to entrench, fortifying some houses and localities and preparing machine gun emplacements. They also assisted to hold the line on HILL 70.

(g) About 9.30 a.m. the 74th Company sent forward to prepare three artillery routes over the German trenches into LOOS and subsequently to near G.30.a. and c.

The routes prepared were :-

    (i) BETHUNE-LENS Road.

    (ii) VERMELLES-LOOS Road.

    (iii) A track in prolongation of a line of bridges previously prepared over our own trenches between (i) and (ii).

(h) The 180th Company were ordered to assist the 74th Coy in the above work. A portion of this company was placed at the disposal of the Divisional Bombing Officer and was employed in the transport of bombs to the assaulting lines.

(i) At 5 p.m. information was received that our Infantry were entrenching on HILL 70, and five pontoon wagons loaded with picks, shovels, sandbags, wire, etc were sent to LOOS and placed at disposal of 46th Infantry Brigade.

26th Sept.

5.

(a) The 73rd Company which had lost all its officers except the Commanding Officer, was ordered back to MAZINGARBE by the G.O.C. 44th Infantry Brigade. Having been reorganised into two sections it rejoined the 44th Infantry Brigade at QUALITY STREET early in the afternoon. This Company, although very exhausted, worked on improving the LENS Road from midnight 26th/27th until the work was completed about 4 a.m. on the 27th.

(b) Two sections of the 91st Company were ordered back to

MAZINGARBE /

MAZINGARBE during the afternoon to rest, but an order being received for every available man to be sent up to the German front trenches they were ordered up again after a very short rest and assisted in collecting numerous stragglers and getting them into the trenches. The remaining portion of the company remained in the neighbourhood of HILL 70 and LOOS during the day, assisting the infantry by every possible means, by holding portions of the firing line improving trenches, collecting and reforming stragglers, and in certain cases were instrumental in checking the retirement of infantry and saved a complete withdrawal from HILL 70.

(c) All available men of 74th and 180th Companies were employed until about 11 a.m. on improving the LOOS Road which was in a very bad condition owing to having been much cut up by shell fire and by trenches dug across it, its condition being rendered worse by the heavy rain which had recently fallen.

(d) At 10.40 a.m. orders were sent to 74th Company to concentrate all these parties near our old front line trenches, to be prepared to block the communication trenches which connected our lines with the German lines and to prepare and restore and improve our wire. All these parties subsequently assisted to prepare the German front and support trenches for defence under the orders of G.O.C. 45th I.B.

(e) The detached section of the 180th Company R.E. joined during the afternoon and was also employed on this work. All remaining tools in MAZINGARBE were sent forward for the use of the troops and stragglers collected in these trenches.

(f) During the night the C.R.E. proceeded to LOOS to

inspect the road, and at midnight the 74th and 73rd Companies, although all very exhausted, were ordered out to do further work on the road which was made passable for motor ambulances by about 4 a.m. on the 27th.

27th September. 6. The Infantry Brigades having been withdrawn the three Field Companies concentrated at LE SAULCHOY Fm, MAZINGARBE. The 180th Company were ordered back into billets at VERQUIN and came under orders of the 4th Corps.

28th September. 7. All units withdrew from MAZINGARBE.

8. During the whole period from 21st September, four men of the 74th Company were employed on water supply duties in Fosse 7 until relieved on the evening of the 28th.

9. The total losses reported during the period under report were:-

    73rd Fd. Coy.   5 Officers.   80 Other Ranks.
    74th Fd. Coy.   14 Other Ranks.
    91st Fd. Coy.   1 Officer.   51 Other Ranks.
    180th (T) Coy.   17 Other Ranks.

The Field Companies went into action with six officers and about 140 other ranks each.

10. Special cases of gallantry and good work are being brought to notice in a separate report. All reports received from independent sources testify to the extremely high standard of discipline, bravery, coolness and resource displayed by all ranks.

(sd) G.S.CARTWRIGHT.

Lt.Col.R.E.,

1/10/15.   C.R.E., 15th Division.

R.E.(2).

15th Division.

In forwarding the attached A.F. W.3121 in connection with the recent operations, I wish to bring to notice the good work carried out by R.E. Companies in the 15th Division, viz:- 73rd, 74th and 91st Field Companies, also the 180th Company, which was attached to the Division before and during this period.

Preparatory Work.

In the preparation of the trenches prior to the assault, the following works were carried out by and under the supervision of the R.E. companies and 9th Gordon Hdrs. aided by large infantry working parties:-

Communications.-

Communication trenches - Northern Up, Southern Up - extension of 12 - 12.A, 22, 23, 29, 31, 32, 16.a., extension of 6, 9.X., and 8.d.

Reserve Trenches.-

Trenches 20 and 21 with a certain number of bays provided with splinter proof covers.

No.24 Reserve Trench.

All trenches were labelled and boards with numbers provided at all junctions, etc., an evacuation trench for the wounded was dug during the 3 last days before the bombardment.

83 recesses were constructed in the parapet of the front trench for gas cylinders.

5 Russian Saps were run out to assist in connecting up the German trenches with our own system after the assault, these had just before the bombardment been carried about 40x to 60x out.

Advanced report centres for 2 Divisional and 3 Brigade Headquarters were provided with bomb-proof shelters.

A trench tramway was laid to assist in the transport of stores from MAZINGARBE to QUALITY STREET.

3 Advanced Dressing Stations were installed at Fosse 7, BREWERY PHILOSOPHE, and ABATTOIR, MAZINGARBE.

Some 26 bridges were built over trenches to allow of transport proceeding along the road and Artillery crossing the trenches.

A number of regimental first aid posts were made in the trenches - off the evacuation trench and near the junction of main communications.

Store depots were also formed in the trenches and in QUALITY STREET and trestle wagons were held in readiness to push forward wire, sandbags, tools, etc., should the opportunity arise.

The reserve store was formed in MAZINGARBE.

Water Supply.

This presented many difficulties but owing to the ingenuity of 2/Lt. Evans and the hard work and perseverance of some 8 or 9 men of the 74th Company, R.E., a pump driven by a petrol engine was made up out of assorted machinery taken out of various places. This pumped about 2,000 gallons per hour out of a well 100 feet deep in Fosse 7. Storage in the trenches was provided by placing 10 galvanised tanks in the reserve trenches and also about 300 petrol tins.

The dressing stations were also provided for in the same manner.

During Operations.

In the attack on 25/9/15, the 73rd Field Coy with "G" Coy, 9th Gordon Highlanders (Pioneers) was with the 44th Brigade, the 74th Company, R.E., 2 Companies (E and F) 9th Gordon Highlanders (Pioneers) and 180th (Tunnelling) Coy, R.E.

/in

in Divisional Reserve and the 91st Field Coy R.E. with "H" Company 9th Gordons with the 46th Brigade.

All ranks displayed great gallantry in carrying out their duties and although they seem to a large extent to have joined in the fighting, yet whenever required they carried out such R.E. works that were called for such as the supervision of the opening up of the Russian Saps and digging communications between our own and the German system of trenches, making crossings for the artillery, repairs to roads to LOOS, assisting the Infantry to entrench on Hill 70, etc.

The 180th Coy R.E. assisted in the constructions of the Russian Saps and during the operations lent great assistance to the 74th Coy R.E. in the consolidation of the German system of trenches, in the repairs to roads, etc.

During the preparatory work and in the actual fighting the conduct and bravery of officers and men in the R.E. Companies was all that could be desired.

The 15th Signal Company, R.E., deserves the greatest credit for their share in the operations. It can, I think, be truly said that the communications throughout were maintained in a very efficient manner and this was entirely due to the unceasing and untiring efforts of all ranks in this unit.

(sd) G.S. CARTWRIGHT. Lt. Col. R.E.
C.R.E., 15th Division.

2/10/15.

9th GORDONS (PIONEERS).

From:
    Colonel W.A. Scott, C.B.,
        Comdg. 9th Gordon Highlanders (Pioneers).

To :
    Headquarters, 15th Division.

I have the honour to report on the part taken by the battalion under my command in the fighting which took place round LOOS on 25th, 26th and 27th September, 1915.

It will be necessary for me to divide the account into four parts, as the battalion was split up:-

1. The part taken by Headqrs. and "E" and "F" Companies.
2. "G" Company which was attached to the 44th Brigade.
3. "H" Company which was attached to the 46th Brigade.
4. The Machine Gun Sections attached to the 44th Brigade.

1. Head-quarters and two companies were ordered to move from NOEUX LES MINES to MAZINGARBE on night of 24th September. At 1 p.m. on 25th September I received an order from Head-quarters 15th Division - "Proceed with your two companies at once to LOOS and place it in a state of defence". The two companies under my command moved off at 1.40 p.m., each man carrying a pick or shovel and six sandbags.

As the BETHUNE - LENS road was being shelled I took a road running south of it, leaving QUALITY STREET and FOSSE 7 on my left (AUCHY - LENS sheet). On reaching the ridge the battalion came under shell fire. I ordered the platoons to extend to three paces and follow one another at 200 paces, the centre of each platoon to move along the road and on reaching LOOS to close and take cover. This was done with very few casualties, though the battalion was shelled the whole way. We reached LOOS at 4.15 p.m. It was being shelled.

                                                  Leaving

Leaving the companies under cover, I went through LOOS to reconnoitre and decided that the east side was the position requiring first attention, as north of it there appeared to be a gap in our line. I could not see where the right of the next division was.

Head-quarters was placed in the main street where it bifurcates, the northern road led to CITE ST. AUGUSTE, the southern to LENS (sheet 36.a.Central). "F" Company I settled should place the building round figure 36 on the left side of the LENS road in defence. "E" Company to make two houses on CITE ST. AUGUSTE road into a keep, and connect with "F" by trenches and prolong the trenches to north of road with the left flank slightly thrown back. This position supported the left of the front line on Hill 70 and might prevent the left flank from being turned.

On going back to the companies Captain Robertson reported he examined some houses and had found 20 German soldiers in them. They were sent to PHILOSOPHE under escort.

At 5 p.m. the companies were ordered to their different positions. Work could not begin till dark on account of the shelling. During the night this work was completed. Continuous shelling went on throughout the night with intermittent bursts of machine-gun fire.

Early in the morning I came to the conclusion the situation was critical, the left flank being entirely unguarded; no British troops could be seen to the north and Germans were firing from PUITS 14 Bis and the copse to the north-west (25.a.). I therefore deemed it advisable not to continue with the defence of LOOS and ordered the two companies to man their defensive positions. During the morning the

the shelling of LOOS was very heavy and considerable numbers of
wounded were coming back from Hill 70, and more and more fire was
coming from the left. At about 1 p.m., I think it was, I noticed
German guns shelling the ridges to my left near where our first
line trenches were. I was much relieved shortly afterwards to
see two battalions in extended order coming up on our left.
They came a certain way and then turned round and retired.
I then managed to find out that Brig.-Gen. Wallerstein, Commanding
45th Brigade, was in LOOS. I went and saw him and explained the
dangerous situation on the left and that it appeared to me from
the machine-gun fire that the Germans were getting more round the
left, and that a considerable number of unwounded men were coming
back. The bombardment of LOOS had also become very violent.
He told me to hang on, as a battalion was on its way up to support
us. They never arrived.

At 3 p.m. I sent the following message to Major MacGregor:-
"Hold on all you can; if forced to retire, do so on German first
line trenches. I am sending up ammunition. Communicate with
Captain Robertson".

I and Head-quarters had to retire down the street to a big
building which appeared to be a German store, as the house I had
been in was knocked nearly flat. At about 4 p.m. I found I could
not get in touch with my two companies. It appears that some
officer in the front line had given the order to "retire".
Afterwards the O.C. "E" Co. reported to me that a man dressed as
a serjeant of the A. & S. Highlanders had come to him and given
him verbal orders to retire from the brigade. He said another
man had been sent to the first line and asked how he could get
there in case the first man failed. Just after he said this
there was a backward movement from Hill 70 and this man then said
"That is all right, he has got there and they are retiring". The
companies then retired. At this time LOOS was a perfect hell of

shell

shell and machine-gun fire, all the streets from the north were being enfiladed. I could not find the Brigadier, and as I could do nothing more, I with Head-quarters retired. I ordered the men to follow me in single file at 5 paces, and by hugging the lee side of the street we managed to get to the trenches with the loss of one man killed and three wounded.

Major MacGregor, after the two companies got to the trenches thought that the order to retire was wrong, and as the fire had considerably modified he ordered the two companies to advance and re-occupy the trenches. This was successfully performed and the firing almost ceased.

At 8 p.m. they were reinforced by a dismounted regiment of cavalry, of the 3rd Cavalry Division. They remained with the cavalry all night and were withdrawn from action on Monday morning.

2. REPORT BY OFFICER COMMANDING "C" COMPANY, ATTACHED TO 44th BRIGADE.

To - Colonel Scott, C.B.,
    Commanding 9th Gordon Highlanders.

Sir,
I have the honour to report the following facts concerning the work done by the company under my command during the operations September 25th-27th.

1. In accordance with orders received two platoons, Nos. 11 and 12, under command of 2nd Lieut. K.B. Kershaw and 2nd Lieut. J. Usher, proceeded on the night of Sept. 24th/25th to trenches in the front line, with instructions to follow the rear companies of the 9th Black Watch and 8th Seaforth Highlanders respectively, as part of the assaulting column.

The other two platoons were ordered to follow in rear of the last battalion of the 44th Brigade.

Company

Company Headquarters with Brigade Headquarters.

2. No. 11 Platoon followed the 6th or 7th line of the Black Watch. Seeing that the left flank of the Black Watch was exposed, Lt. Kershaw led his platoon half left and took some German trenches immediately on the left of the Black Watch. At this time the Black Watch had not yet reached the German first line trenches and were under a hot fire from machine guns, rifles and bombs.

The second line was captured without opposition and an advance made on LOOS.

Within 300 yards of LOOS where a road crosses the front, a hot fire was encountered from machine guns. Lieut Kershaw was killed at this point, after having been previously wounded in the arm. All accounts agree that this officer performed most gallantly in leading that part of the line to the assault on LOOS.

Serjeant Findlay then led the platoon into LOOS, where, with the aid of a very gallant Cameron Highlander who threw bombs, a house was captured from which machine gun fire was coming, and 40 or 50 Germans forced to surrender.

The platoon then advanced on to Hill 70 which they helped to consolidate.

3. No 12 Platoon followed behind the Seaforth Highlanders till within 200 yards of LOOS. As by this time they had 12 casualties and the front line was held up at the barbed wire, Lieut Usher joined the firing line. LOOS was stormed. In the town Lieut Usher found several civilians and at once sent them back under escort to QUALITY STREET. LOOS being taken an advance was made on Hill 70. Hill 70 was passed and the line advanced some 300 yards beyond the redoubt almost to CITE ST AUGUSTE. Lt Usher did very good work here

/showing

showing a fine example of fearlessness under a hot enfilade fire.

Eventually the line there was forced to retire as the right had been driven back. During the retirement, while fighting a rear-guard action, the platoon lost heavily Lieut Usher being killed. On Hill 70 he was as cool as if he was on parade, cheering up the men in every way. He stopped one retirement, and had supports arrived in time, Hill 70 would have been saved. Serjeant McKIMMIE took over command and retired with the few men left through the redoubt. He then did some excellent work bringing up tools and wire from a German store in LOOS to the firing line and issued them to troops passing through. He then dug a line between the two roads going over Hill 70 with the aid of some leaderless men, which line eventually became part of the line held that night.

4. Nos. 9 and 10 Platoons under Lieut. ROBERTSON-DURHAM and Lieut. STEEDMAN, after the assaulting column had gone on started to open up the new saps from the front line to the enemy's line, under a heavy shell fire. Both platoons lost heavily during this, losing 20% of their men.

They were ordered then to follow behind the 10th Gordon Highlanders and eventually reach HILL 70. Both the platoons passed the redoubt and when the first line retired, Lieut STEEDMAN held on to the redoubt with a mixed lot of men for some considerable time.

Lieut ROBERTSON-DURHAM did good work consolidating and strengthening the reverse slope of the Hill after the redoubt was lost, and when found on the extreme left had his men dug in and sentries posted. He crossed over from the right to the left on their retirement from the top of Hill 70, considering rightly that that was the exposed and therefore dangerous flank.

/The

The Company was ordered by the General Officer Commanding 44th Brigade to be withdrawn at 5.p.m., and this was accomplished by the Officer Commanding Company after the line had been reorganised under cover of darkness. The Company passed through LOOS about 10 p.m. and, Brigade Headquarters having been withdrawn to QUALITY STREET, was taken back to that point, some 80 strong, where it went into Brigade Reserve.

Next day at 3 p.m. orders were received to hold the original support line trenches, and next day, September 27th, the company was withdrawn with the rest of the battalion and the 44th Infantry Brigade to MAZINGARBE.

The Company went into action some 205 strong and its casualties were:-

    Killed - 8 Other Ranks and 2 Officers.
    Wounded - 73 Other ranks.
    Wounded and
    Missing - 7 Other Ranks.
    Missing 25 Other Ranks. ⌀

    Total - 103 Other Ranks and 2 Officers. *

⌀ Mostly hit beyond Hill 70.
* 2nd/Lt. KERSHAW and 2nd/Lt. ROBERTSON-DURHAM.

3. "H" Company lost all its officers and senior Serjts; only two Serjeants came out of action unwounded. The senior Serjeant, Serjeant Merry, compiled these notes:-

"H" Company, 9th Gordon Highlanders (Pioneers).
Report by Serjeant Merry.

On the morning of the 25th the company was divided as follows:-

No. 13 Platoon, under 2nd/Lt. Murray, was attached to 10th Scottish Rifles.

No.14 Platoon, under 2nd/Lt. Bisset, was ordered to support No.13 Platoon.

No.15 Platoon, under 2nd/Lt PITCAIRN, was attached to 7th King's Own Scottish Borderers.

No.16 Platoon, under 2nd/Lt. MACGREGOR, was ordered to support No.15 Platoon.

Each platoon was ordered to proceed to the fire trench by a different route, but on arrival there, owing to some slight confusion, each platoon at once became a fighting unit and attached itself to the nearest line and advanced with them to German first line trenches. 2nd/Lt. PITCAIRN was wounded just before reaching the German trench, and his Platoon, No.15 suffered very severely about the same time. The remainder of the company continued the advance with the nearest unit in the direction of Hill 70.

About this point, Captain MACWHIRTER, finding the line again getting into confusion, re-organised the remainder of 15 and 16 Platoons and men of other Corps in his immediate vicinity, and named them 9th Gordons and took command of same.

At the same time, 2nd/Lt. MURRAY performed a similar service in his part of the line and placed them in charge of Serjeant Merry.

2nd Lieut MURRAY seeing that there were no officers in charge of the line in front of him, went forward and took charge and advanced with them to reinforce the firing line.

Captain MACWHIRTER's command continued the advance until it reached the LA BASSEE - LENS Road, where they were ordered to dig themselves in. This happened at about 4 p.m., but at 8 p.m. they were ordered to advance North along the said Road for about 800 yards and again dig in and to hold that position. This was held till about 11 a.m. on the 26th.

About this time Captain MACWHIRTER, seeing the troops on his right and also some of the 15th Division on his left were retiring, rallied his men and encouraged them to hold on

/and

and try to cover the retirement. The enemy then concentrated their machine gun and rifle fire on this party and forced them to retire. This was carried out at a steady pace under orders of Captain MACWHIRTER, during which, Captain MACWHIRTER was wounded in the hand. 2nd Lieut. MACGREGGOR was killed and Serjeant BLACK and Serjeant MITCHELL were wounded.

The line again became confused owing to the enemy's heavy fire, but as soon as cover was reached Corporal McCULLY gathered as many of the 9th Gordons as he could find and was then ordered by General WILKINSON to report to Captain TAYLOR at Headquarters in QUALITY STREET.

The men under command of 2nd Lieut MURRAY, supported by Serjeant MERRY's command, continued to advance over Hill 70 but were forced to retire to a bank about 250 yards in rear, where they remained until reinforced. During this retirement there was again much confusion, but Captain LONGMAN of the 10th Gordons, assisted by Lieuts STEEDMAN and ROBERTSON-DURHAM, Company Serjeant Major ERRIDGE and Serjeant ROBSON, checked the retirement and re-organised the line.

Shortly afterwards, 2nd/Lt. MURRAY rejoined the line and again retold off in sections and commenced to dig in. During this time 2nd/Lt. MURRAY was wounded across the back by a machine gun bullet, but he remained with his command until he saw that every man was safely dug in, when he handed over to Serjeant MERRY, he then retired to the Dressing Station.

This party then remained in this position until about 10 p.m. when they were ordered to retire and report to Capt. TAYLOR, this being carried out without further loss. The total strength of this company then gathered together by Serjeant MERRY numbered 30 N.C.O's and men.

- 10 -

4. MACHINE GUN SECTIONS.

It is extremely difficult to find out exactly the part taken by the Machine Guns of the Battalions as Lieut ALLAN, the Machine Gun Officer, was killed on the East side of Hill 70 and all the N.C.O's were killed or wounded.

At first they were ordered to occupy Sap 18 and bring fire on the LENS Road Redoubt, after the capture of which they were to move forward and act as circumstances occurred. After leaving Sap 18 they went forward through LOOS and came into action on Hill 70 on the crest of the Hill, having the German redoubt on their left. They then advanced again and came into action at close range of CITE St AUGUSTE, this was about 9.30 a.m. About 1.30 p.m. the line was forced to retire. It is believed that Lieut ALLAN was killed here, as he could not be found, and Serjeant WATSON gave the order to retire. They were nearly the last to go. The men crawled back extended, with the guns dismantled. They appear to have made another stand on the East side of Hill 70. Serjeant MACDOWALL, who appears to have been with the reserve section, went forward to see the situation. He never returned and the machine guns and their gunners were never seen on the West side of the hill. It is believed that the guns were destroyed and the gunners with them killed or wounded in retiring over the crest. Corporal MACKAY, though severely wounded, continued to take up ammunition to the guns. He was last seen lying by the road on West side of Hill 70. After the guns were lost the remainder of the section and reserve section were employed as riflemen.

It has been brought to my notice by several officers that the Machine Gun Section, under Lieut ALLAN and Serjeant WATSON, fought and behaved in a most exemplary manner; they fought their guns until both guns and gunners were wiped out.

(sd) W.A.SCOTT. Colonel.
1/10/15.   Comdg 9th Gordon Highlanders(Pioneers

Div. Mounted Troops.

Report on Operations September 24th to 28th.
15th Divisional Mounted Troops.

September 24th. 7 p.m. Squadron moved up to NOEUX LES MINES and bivouaced there.

3 Platoons Cyclists and M.M.G.Battery to dug-outs prepared behind MAZINGARBE, O.C.Mounted Troops with them.

Remainder of Cyclists under A.P.M.

September 25th.
10.30 a.m. Orders received for 11th M.M.G.Battery to proceed to QUALITY STREET to report to 44th Infantry Brigade. They are to be moved forward later to Northern outskirts of LOOS at discretion of G.O.C. 44th Infantry Brigade with a view to support our attack on Hill 70.

In answer to further enquiries they are instructed to take no Cyclists with them and to leave F.Trench Mortar Battery at MAZINGARBE.

They started off at 11.10. The O.C. 11th M.M.G. Battery reports their further progress.

11.45. Orders received for 2 Platoons of Cyclists to get ready and for O.C.Cyclists to report to Div. H.Q.

They started off about mid-day. O.C.Cyclists reports their further progress.

11.50. Orders received for Squadron to move up to join me at MAZINGARBE.

They arrived at 1.30 having been much hindered on the road full of cavalry and supporting troops.

12.0 mid-day. Thousands of cavalry passed between NOYELLES - MAZINGARBE, continuous stream for more than an hour.

21st Division begins to arrive from NOEUX LES MINES and form up in L.16.b. and L.16.c. just behind our position and halt there.

/Squadron

Squadron complete and 1 Platoon of Cyclists stand by for orders for remainder of day.

12 midnight. F.Trench Mortar was ordered to report to 46th Infantry Brigade LOOS.

September 26th. 11.30 a.m. Remaining platoon of cyclists sent for to assist battle police.

12. mid-day. One troop of cavalry ordered to report to A.P.M. for escort and road control work. Dispatch No.1 Troops at 12.15. They remained out till 6 p.m. Sept.27th.

4 p.m. Orders received that remainder of squadron was to go out and work under 44th Infantry Brigade dismounted. Rode up to Fosse 7 and sent back horses from there. Report to 44th Infantry Brigade in QUALITY STREET at 5.15 p.m. with 57 men.

6.15 p.m. Carry entrenching tools to O.C. 7th Camerons and 10th Gordons. Take up 100 picks and 100 shovels in two journeys to original German trenches on LENS Road.

8 p.m. Carry rations to Brigade Headquarters and send party with rations to 10th Gordons in old German trenches near LENS Road.

10 p.m. Unload a lorry of smoke helmets at R.E. Stores, QUALITY STREET.

Midnight. C.R.E. asks for 20 men to assist in repairing LENS Road, sent troops up under S/Lt. Burns Lindow.

September 27th. 2.30 a.m. Orders received at Brigade Headquarters that the Division is to come out to billets in MAZINGARBE. Marched back to dug-outs at L.17.c. arriving there at 4 a.m.

9 a.m. Find M.M.G.Battery has returned during our absence. O.C.Cyclist Company with two Platoons returns during the morning.

/6 p.m.

6 p.m. No.1 Troop returned from A.P.M. also Platoon of Cyclists.

10 p.m. Sent for to 1st Divisional Headquarters and receive orders to be ready to move at one hour's notice with all available mounted troops. Order cancelled at 9.30 a.m. September 29th and mounted troops ordered to march to billets at DROUVIN.

September 28th. 12.30 a.m. Ordered to send out two officers patrols to find position of captured German Field Guns in LOOS. 2/Lt. Robinson and Burns Lindow went out but found themselves in the middle of the Guards Division who were advancing towards LOOS and were unable to make progress before dark. They returned not having discovered the guns, having been held up by the heavy bombardment directed against the Guards Division till the light gave out.

They were instructed to be ready to start again at dawn but the orders were subsequently cancelled.

(sd) J.W.CROPPER. Major,
1/10/15. O.C., 15th Divisonal Mounted Troops.

15th Divisional Cyclist Company.
Report on action 25th/26th and 27th September 1915.

1. Distribution of Company.

On 24th September the Company was distributed as follows:-

In dug-outs in MAZINGARBE. Headquarters and 3 platoons and one officer, and one section of another platoon.

On control posts. 2 Platoons (less 1 officer and 1 section).

Escort to Prisoners. One Platoon.

2. First order to move.

At about 11.45 a.m. on 25th received orders to send two platoons to LOOS and for the commander to report to Adv. Divl. Headquarters for instructions. I therefore reported in person to Divisional Headquarters and was ordered to report to G.O.C. 46th Infantry Brigade and to instruct the O.C. 11th M.M.G.Battery to do the same.

As exact position of H.Q. 46th Infantry Brigade was not known, I was instructed to go to the church in LOOS, where an orderly would meet me with further orders. However, on reaching the church no orderly was to be found and the vicinity was being very heavily shelled.

3. Progress of the detachment to LOOS.

On passing through QUALITY STREET was told by an officer that we were urgently required so pushed on as quickly as possible.

At the German front line trenches the mud on the LENS Road was so bad that cycles had to be carried. This delayed matters.

The 11th M.M.G.Battery were likewise affected. I found O.C.Battery and told him we were both to report to G.O.C. 46th Brigade.

/After

After reforming my leading Platoon we pushed on and soon after turning off the LENS Road came under rifle fire. I increased the pace and got under cover of a wall in the outskirts of LOOS. Two men were hit and the rear had to take cover from shell fire. Only a small party arrived in LOOS with me.

4. Advance through LOOS.

Shortly after arrival in LOOS No.2 Section 11th M.M.G. Battery under Lieut. Mc.Farlane came up carrying their guns and some ammunition. I therefore left one of my officers 2/Lt. Duncan to reform my detachment, told off all the men with me to help carry guns, etc., for No.2. Section M.M.G. Battery and advanced through LOOS.

Lt. Mc.Farlane went on to reconnoitre and I verified position by map. Having arrived at the situation, I sent them on and the party with the two guns got established in the front line on Hill 70.

I went back to bring up the remainder of my detachment and also collected some odd men of No.2 Section M.M.G.Battery who had a hand cart with ammunition. We went forward through Loos and I halted the party under a bank 100x in rear of the support line and went on to reconnoitre and ascertain the situation.

5. Reconnaissance on Hill 70.

On reaching the firing line about the centre of the Hill, I found that all units of the Division were mixed up. I reported to several Commanding Officers but could not find one of the 46th Brigade. As our lines on the Hill were crowded with men, I consulted O.C.7th Camerons as to advisability of withdrawing my detachment, after ascertaining what

/the

the situation was on the left. I went along our line to the left discussing the situation with officers on route and finally reached the LA BASSEE - LENS Road about 400x South of PUITS 14 Bis where I found a detachment of about 100 7th Royal Scots Fus., this flank appeared to be rather in the air and was being shelled by our own guns. I wrote a message to O.C., 7th Camerons explaining the situation and took it back part of the way myself.

Then returned to my detachment, left a squad under Serjt. Scott to assist No.2 Section M.M.G.Battery, sent an officers patrol under 2/Lt. Duncan by a less exposed route further over to the left to join touch with the 2nd Brigade; ordered one platoon under 2/Lt. Chubb to withdraw to a communication trench near LOOS CEMETERY and went back myself to report.

6. LOOS.

Met G.S.O.2 of 15th Division, explained what I knew of situation. He wrote message which was despatched in duplicate by four of 2/Lt. Chubb's Platoons back to Divisional Headquarters.

Received no further orders but was instructed to remain in LOOS. Distribution of Cyclist detachment was then as follows:-

    2/Lt. Chubb's Platoon, more or less complete in communication trench near LOOS CEMETERY.

    2/Lt. Duncan out with a patrol to left of 15th Div. One squad of his platoon on Hill 70 with No.2.Section M.M.G.Battery, another with No.1 Section M.M.G. Battery in trench near LOOS CEMETERY.

The remainder with me as orderlies.

I attached myself to Headquarters 44th Brigade and later to 45th Brigade, when G.O.C. 45th Brigade took over the

/line

line and endeavoured to assist with guides and messengers.

At about 9 p.m. as a number of messengers, etc., were constantly being required, I got 2/Lt. Chubb's Platoon established in a cellar in LOOS. 2/Lt. Duncan reported that he had got in touch with 2nd Infantry Brigade on our left and had explained how our line was situated. As the Officer i/c No.1 Section M.M.G.Battery had been wounded, I ordered him to take over command of their section. Later, ammunition was required by firing line on Hill 70 and 2/Lt Chubb with his Platoon made numerous trips throughout the night and early morning of the next day 26th.

The situation remained the same until early in the afternoon.

My detachment got still further split up owing to a party of 2/Lt. Chubb's platoon, who got separated, being ordered by a medical officer to act as stretcher bearers and I decided to withdraw and reform. 2nd Lt. Duncan brought out No.1 Section M.M.G.Battery from the trenches that was being heavily shelled and succeeded in bringing them back under heavy fire.

7. <u>Behind the line.</u>

I reported to Divisional H.Q. about 4 p.m. on 26th for further orders and was instructed to reform and collect as many men of the company as possible and report to G.O.C. 46th Infantry Brigade at LOOS ROAD KEEP taking up all stragglers with me.

I was ordered by G.O.C.46th Infantry Brigade to halt near QUALITY STREET.

On the morning of 27th I handed over the stragglers which I had collected and about 11.30 a.m. received orders

/to

to withdraw to billets in MAZINGARBE.

8.   Recommendations.

I would like to bring to your notice the names of the following officers and N.C.O. :-

2/Lt. R.N.CHUBB, who made numerous journeys through LOOS under heavy artillery fire, taking up ammunition through the firing line on HILL 70.

2/Lt. T.H.DUNCAN who successfully carried out a reconnaissance and got in touch with 2nd Infantry Brigade under fire, and later took command of No.1 Section M.M.G. Battery.

No.1595 Serjeant F.SCOTT., who greatly assisted No.2 Section M.M.G.Battery on Hill 70, remaining there until both guns were disabled.

(sd) J.C.COOKE. Capt.
Commanding 15th Divisional Cyclist Coy.

1/10/15.

Report from 11th Motor Machine Gun Battery - Operations
September 21st to 30th, 1915.

To O.C., Divisional Mounted Troops.

I beg to report as follows:-

1.   September 21st to 23rd inclusive. Continued preparing dug-outs at the base allotted to this battery in L.17.b. 4.4. (1/40,000. 36.b).

2.   September 24th. Received orders to remove battery to above base. Started from VAUDRICOURT 8.10 p.m. arrived 8.35 p.m.

3.   September 25th. Informed I was under direct orders of D.H.Q., but received through you, at 10.20 a.m., an order to report to 44th Infantry Brigade Headquarters. Started at 11.10 a.m., 4 officers, 54 O.R., 8 Sole Cycles, 19 Cycles with side cars, 4 box cars, 8 guns, 85,000 rounds S.A.A.

Arrived QUALITY STREET 11.20 a.m., G.O.C.44th Infantry Brigade was on the road. Halted battery for one minute only. Received verbal order "take your guns to LOOS and help support us on Hill 70, if you can get them there - the road is not yet bridged".

4.   Progress along the LENS Road was fair until our second line trench. From thereonwards the clay bogged the wheels and progress was very difficult. At each trench I waited until a party of the 74th Field Coy R.E. had bridged by filling in. I was forced to dismount my men and push and lift the cycles over the impossible places. I went forward and found the road beyond the German trenches in good condition and the LOOS Cemetery Road quite good.

5.   It being now 12.30 p.m. I gave the order for the

/guns

guns to advance in the handcarts. This order was received after 5 sidecars had been pushed over 250 yards of mud, etc. So that the guns of Nos 1 and 2 Sections came on their cycles. At the cemetery the road was crossed by a trench. We tried to bridge this with wooden tombstones, but it would not carry the cycles so I left them under fair cover by the road side. The guns went forward, being carried. No 3 Section quickly followed with guns in hand carts. No.2 was the reserve section but rushed on and I put No.1 in reserve at the cemetery trenches.

6. Capt Cooke, 15th Divisional Cyclists, met me at the junction of LENS and LOOS Roads, bearing instructions for me to report to 48th Infantry Brigade. He then proceeded promising the aid of some of his men to carry ammunition for my sections, as we were on foot. His detachment followed him 400 yards in rear. I warned these men and other supports to the side of the road as rifle fire down the road was lively. Capt Cooke gave me very valuable aid in personally guiding one of my sections and some of my men, sent up later, to Hill 70.

7. The LENS Road was being shelled, 1.30 p.m., and I returned to my cycles and cars. With the assistance of the remaining men all the cycles and cars were moved back over the crest of the Hill and left on the side of the road, leaving the road quite clear for traffic.

8. At 3 p.m. I received a fifth box car.

9. No.3 Section with two guns reached a position on the North of the mine dump G.36.d.9.3. early in the afternoon and

/by

by 4.30 p.m. had dug themselves in. Royal Scots and some Camerons were in this trench. The 18th London Irish dug a support trench 150 yards in rear. It is a good trench. During the evening the East Yorks reinforced the front line.

September 26th. It was fairly quiet until 2 a.m. when fast fighting began and lasted through the dawn. My guns fired about 8,000 rounds each. During the British attack, beginning at 9 a.m., my guns kept up overhead fire, which proved effective. The Royal Scots charged successfully 3 times but received no support from the East Yorks.

At 3 p.m. my men being exhausted and the belts being wet and difficult to fill to prove effective, the Major i/c the trench ordered the section to evacuate, which it did, picking up the cycles at the cemetery and returning along the LENS Road, meeting a party with a box car which I had sent forward to find them.

10.   2nd Lt. C.O.D. Anderson commanding No.3 Section and I beg to call attention to his commendable services and very gallant conduct. By request he looked after other M.G's in the trench. He was also responsible for the barricades and guards on the mine dump which effectively stopped the enfilading. With the assistance of an officer of the 18th London, he stopped a stampede of the East Yorks. He started a communication trench between front and support lines but the fire was too intense. He brought his guns and men out safely under heavy fire and trying circumstances.

11.   No. 2 Section got their guns in position on the N. of the sunken road early in the afternoon and dug in with the 10th Gordons and other troops. It was not a trench but a succession of small pits. Five Lewis guns were there also.

/By

By request, Lt. MacFarlane of my Battery looked after these guns. The left flank especially was being enfiladed and a trench was therefore dug 60 yards below the crest of the Hill and the line retired to it at 8 p.m. 25th. Rapid fire began at 8 a.m. and continued intermittently until 7 a.m. 26th. Late in the afternoon of 25th Capt Cooke guided some of my men with ammunition to No.2 Section. At 5 a.m. the Northumberland Fusiliers relieved the 10th Gordons. At 8 a.m. our artillery opened fire but for some time practically shelled our trench. The left of our line had, for a period, to evacuate. At 9 a.m. our line attacked. Major Hall, Northumberlands, ordered the machine guns to also advance. The Infantry returned hurriedly and the guns were with difficulty brought back. Major Hall, Northumberlands, was wounded in the first assault.

6 more assaults were attempted but the majority of the battalion did not participate. The ridge was carried several times but enough men could not be got up to hold it. It was in the fourth attack that Lt. MacFarlane was mortally wounded. He rallied the Northumberlands, stood on the parapet to encourage them and led them for 25 yards when he fell, one of my gunners and two cyclists carried him into the trench and later to the dressing station at LOOS. Serjt. E.N.G.White of No.2 Section took command and was assisted by Serjt Scott and six cyclists in working the guns. The guns gave the infantry plenty of support. Serjt Scott, Cyclists, was also instrumental in rallying the Infantry and behaved most gallantly.

About 3 p.m. one of my guns was smashed by a bullet and shortly after the other jammed. The guns were ordered out of action and retired.

12.   Lieut. Macfarlane and Serjeant E.N.G.White. The work of this officer and N.C.O. are worthy of attention. They both behaved most gallantly, and Lt Macfarlane, if he had stayed by his gun, instead of so bravely helping the situation, might have been alive to-day.

13.   No.1 Section unfortunately lost its commander Capt B.Arthur on the afternoon of 25th. He was wounded in the thigh by shrapnel while sitting in a trench at LOOS Cemetery. He was taken safely back to the base and evacuated. O.C. Cyclists kindly lent me 2/Lt Duncan who had passed a Vickers course at the 15th Divl. M.G.School. He took charge of No.1 Section for me. This section was always in reserve in good machine gun positions with alternative positions ready.

14.   To bring safely the guns, men and M.T. out of action looked like a problem as a machine gun was playing on the Cemetery Road and the LENS Road was being shelled, however, it proved an easy, though extended matter. By making several trips with the box cars I was able to man the serviceable cycles and tow the damaged ones. A majority I got out in the early hours of the 27th. By 9 a.m. 27th I had all my men (excepting casualties) and all M.T. excepting one Douglas Solo, which was borrowed by a 1st Divisional Despatch Rider and has not been returned.

14.   Battery Serjeant Major David H.Hord rendered valuable assistance and behaved most gallantly under the trying circumstances of extricating men and M.T. He also assisted me splendidly during the night 25/26 when an endeavour was made to straighten out the transport tangle at the LENS ROAD Redoubt.

15. Casualties - Lieut. Macfarlane killed, Captain Arthur and 1 O.R. wounded. 2 O.R. were slightly wounded but continued on duty. 6 men were gassed by the gas shells on morning of 26th due to them not having their smoke helmets ready for instant service. They recovered in a few hours. The box covers of three cars were struck by bullets and shrapnel but the damage is practically nil. 11 bicycles and side cars were hit by shrapnel. Three were so badly damaged that on the 27th I loaded them into the box cars and sent them to repair shop at AUCHEL. The others were repaired by my own fitters, who also repaired the one gun damaged.

16. Communication I found good except that at times it was very difficult to find the H.Q. desired or a working telephone. Communication was kept up with my section throughout the night 25/26 by men from my battery on foot. No.3 Section, after retiring to support trench, was out of touch and not returning to the rendezvous for some time, was reported missing. My searching party eventually met the section on the LENS Road.

17. A feature of our work was the usefulness of the hand carts, which the G.O.C. allowed me to have made. These were also used in taking ammunition to Hill 70 for the 44th Infantry Brigade.

18. September 27th. Entire battery occupied in cleaning and repairing.

19. September 28th. Stood by ready to move at one hour notice as per orders received at midnight 27/28. At noon received orders to move to DROUVIN. Started 12.45 p.m., arrived 1.10 p.m. Remained in billets.

20. September 29th. Received orders to move to LABUISSIERE, started 4 p.m., arrived 4.30.

21. September 30th. At billets in LABUISSIERE refitting.

22. The enemy troops at Hill 70 were 22nd Regiment, 157th or 153rd and 233rd. The latter shoulder strap had a grenade on it and probably was artillery.

23. There was practically no road control.

24. A sketch map is attached roughly showing my gun positions on Hill 70.

2/10/15. (sd) C.B.HALL. Major.

SKETCH — NOT TO SCALE.

Enemy Working Party

CREST OF HILL 70
(250-300)

† Lewis Guns 4th B.D.P.
X H.M.G Battery Guns
N.R.S. in after charge.
Dig in on 26th.

FIRE TRENCH
Later 4th B Infantry
10th Gordons
Northumberland Fus.
10th Gordons Later
Northumberland Fus.

200 yds

13 R.S.
4 H.M.G
2 Guns
4 Pr 2.5"
Till 10 AM 26th

SUNKEN ROAD

SpH 351

11/5 LONDON

SUPP LINE

M.N.G at 10 AM 26th
Till 3 PM JL

Lot of E.YORKS
Stopped here
& sent back to
FIRE TRENCH.

Guard 8 Men

Barricade 5 Men

Mine Dump

DOUBLE PYLON

Lewis Guns of E.YORKS brought in late in the evening

LOOS

Report on Communications during the fighting at LOOS and
HILL 70, on 25/9/15 and 26/9/15.

1. Preliminary Measures.- The existing wires between
MAZINGARBE, QUALITY STREET, LOOS ROAD KEEP and LENS ROAD
KEEP were improved and fresh wires laid. The existing wire
in the trenches was improved and replaced by new D.S.
The arrangement of the wires is as shewn in the attached
diagram (fig.1).

Of the wires from Divisional Headquarters to the
Headquarters of Brigades:-

One wire - an existing power wire - was buried one
metre 50.

Two were almost entirely in trenches and the remainder were partly in trenches, partly laid across the open
behind rails in ditches or otherwise, both protected from
splinters and traffic and concealed from view.

The weather during the operations was wet and the
ground sodden.

The wires laid in the open and on the sides of
tracks were in many places buried by the weight of heavy
transport moving over and near them. No wires were cut by
traffic but as a result of being so buried in wet ground
it was found impossible to use a ringing telephone on these
lines owing to leakage and on the morning of the 26th a
"poled cable" line was laid between MAZINGARBE and QUALITY
STREET for use as a telephone line.

With lines in the communication trenches little or
no trouble was experienced. It was found that the best
height to lay these was 18 inches above the bottom of the
trench, i.e., knee high. Owing to the chalk in which the

/trenches

trenches were made, grooving was not possible as this
process spoilt the side of the trench. The wire was
stapled on the side of the trench and was held by "staples
long" (obtained from R.E.Field Companies) at intervals of
10 feet, smaller staples being used between these every
foot to 1:6", so as to keep the wire flat against the side
of the trench.

Burying wires in the bottom of trenches was tried
but was found useless as:-

1. It was dug up by working parties improving
the trench.

2. In the rarer cases where not destroyed as in
1. it become sodden and leaking.

3. The labour involved in so burying the wire was
excessive and not justified by the results
obtained.

In addition to communication by wire, provision was
made to employ:-

(a) Visual.

(b) Pigeons.

(c) Wireless.

Figure №2 shows the arrangements made to link up
Divisional Headquarters to Fosse 3, QUALITY STREET and four
visual stations in the trenches.

It was proposed that visual stations should move
forward with the attack but for various reasons very little
use was made of visual.

Artillery Communications.

The G.O.C. R.A. was linked up to the IVth Corps R.A.
his own Brigades and various Brigades attached to him by
lines laid by the Signal Company. A duplicate route was
provided to each Brigade. Ringing telephones to R.A.
Brigades were used as far as possible.

/Wires

Wires were also laid to right and left Infantry Brigades for use by R.A. observing officers with these Brigades.

A detachment from the Signal Company under a subaltern officer (2nd E.R.L.PEAKE) were attached to R.A. Headquarters to lay and maintain these lines and control traffic on them. This arrangement is considered a very satisfactory one.

All lines both for infantry and R.A. were manned during the bombardment which preceded the action and tested every half hour. There were test-points at Divisional Headquarters, LENS ROAD KEEP, QUALITY STREET and MAZINGARBE CHATEAU.

The office at Divisional Headquarters was all prepared and instruments installed so that when the unit arrived at 6 p.m. on 24/9/15, the operators sat down to their instruments and were able to work without further delay.

Work on 24/9/15. Brigade Headquarters moved up on that day from MAZINGARBE CHATEAU and the house prepared as Divisional Headquarters to QUALITY STREET and LOOS ROAD KEEP respectively.

The change took place smoothly, both telegraph and telephone lines being in good order.

Work on 25/9/15. The 45th Brigade Headquarters arrived at LENS Road Keep.

At 5 a.m. representatives of all three brigades were called on the phone, each checked their watches with an officer of the Divisional Staff. Operation Orders were issued over the wire to all brigades.

The attack.- Communication was kept up with 44th Brigade as follows:- QUALITY STREET was put in communication with a dug-out in our No.6 trench which was used as an advanced report centre. From thence messages were sent out by runner or bicycle orderly to LOOS.

/Wires

Wires were laid forward but frequently cut by shell fire.

An attempt to use the wire in the German trenches was frustrated by a British Officer who repeatedly cut the wire.

A line was got through finally to LOOS by the Brigade Section but its existence was precarious. A cable wagon was sent up at 5.45 p.m. and a D.5. line laid to LOOS which worked all through the night.

As regards the 46th Brigade, when Brigade Headquarters moved on to the Headquarters of the 7th K.O.S.Bs, wires were put through to that place.

Two wires were run out during the attack and communication maintained by means of them with the battalions during the day. Runners were only used at intervals when these wires were broken.

The 45th Brigade moved up to QUALITY STREET during the afternoon and used the 44th Brigade office to send and receive messages.

Wires were laid by them to keep in touch with their battalions.

<u>Work on the 26th.</u> During the night 25/26th the 45th Brigade moved up to LOOS and the 44th Brigade back to QUALITY STREET.

It was considered desirable to connect LOOS to Divisional Headquarters by means of a ringing phone. Two cable wagons were sent out at 4.30 a.m. on 26/9/15.

One laid a poled cable line from MAZINGARBE to QUALITY STREET and the other, under Lt. J.F.Chadwick, laid a line from QUALITY STREET to LOOS.

Speaking on these lines was excellent till about 9 a.m. when the wire was cut and in spite of the effort of

/the

the linesmen the shelling was such that neither this line nor the buzzer line to LOOS could be kept "through".

The signal officer at LOOS, Lt.J.F.Ormsby, then made excellent use of the two remaining means of communication at his disposal, viz:-

(a) Pigeons.
(b) Wireless.

Both these were singularly successful and by means of them the G.O.C.15th Division kept Au Fait with the situation at LOOS.

The wireless finally broke down owing to being discovered by a German "jamming" station, which proceeded to drown all its signals.

Shortly after this the Headquarters 45th Brigade was established at QUALITY STREET. Despatch runners from QUALITY STREET to LOOS were also employed to send messages to the 45th Brigade.

Motor Cyclists.- Owing to the bad state of the BETHUNE - LENS Road, East of QUALITY STREET, the use of motor cyclists was well nigh impossible. Two motor cyclists were sent to deliver messages to LOOS on the night 25/26th. They left their bicycles at the top of the crest, East of QUALITY STREET, and then proceeded to LOOS on foot.

Communication with neighbouring units. Wires were used to connect the 15th Division to the 47th and 1st Divisions. Motor Cyclists to communicate with the 21st and 24th Divisions.

General Notes.- 1. Ringing phones were much used in this action. The G.O.C.15th Division being connected up to the brigades as well as to the IVth Corps and neighbouring Divisions (1st and 47th).

(sd) A.HOLMES-SCOTT.
Captain, R.E.,
1/10/15. O.C., 15th Signal Company R.E.

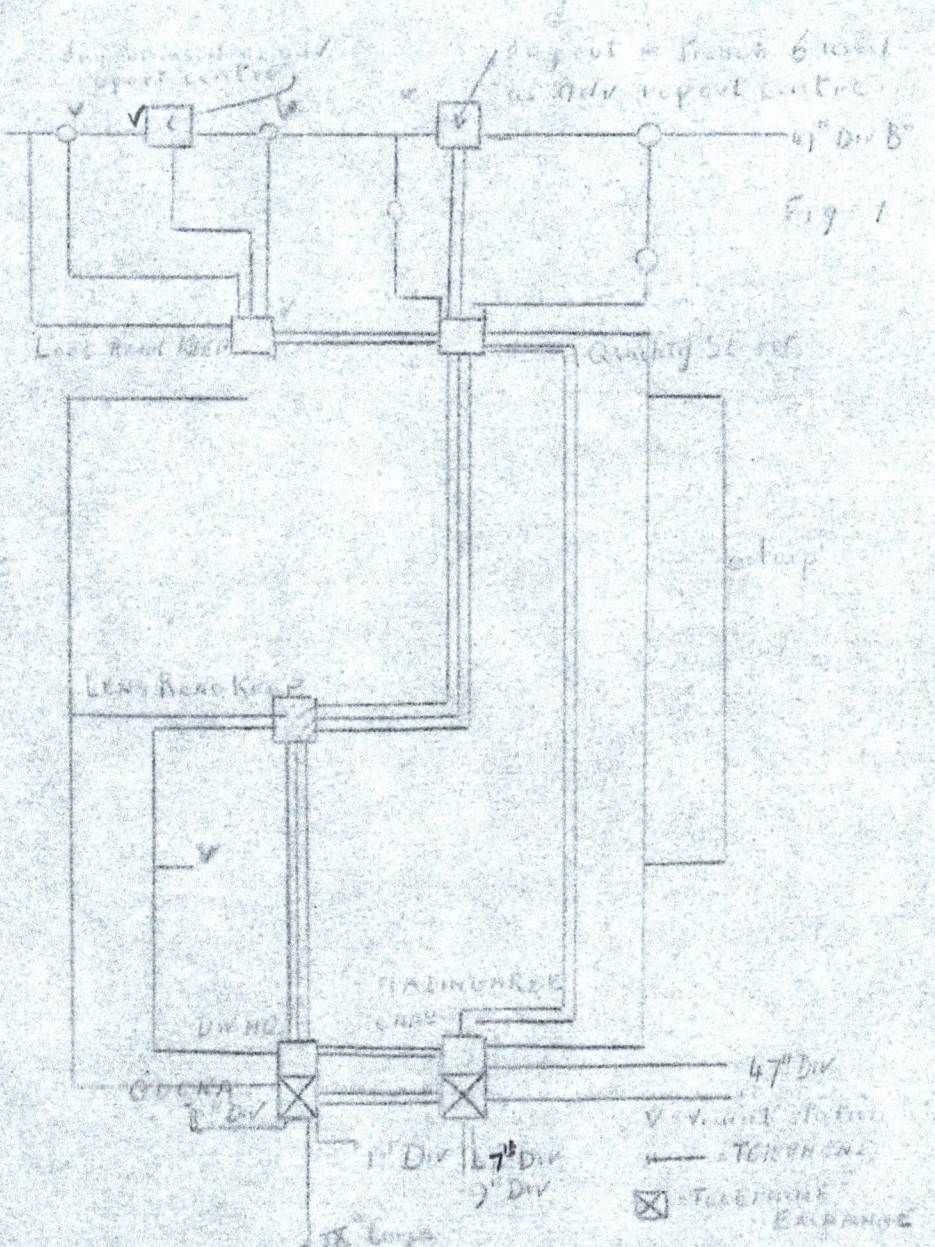

Arrangements for Visual Communication

FIG 2

V3 = Station in Support trenches near Telephone offices

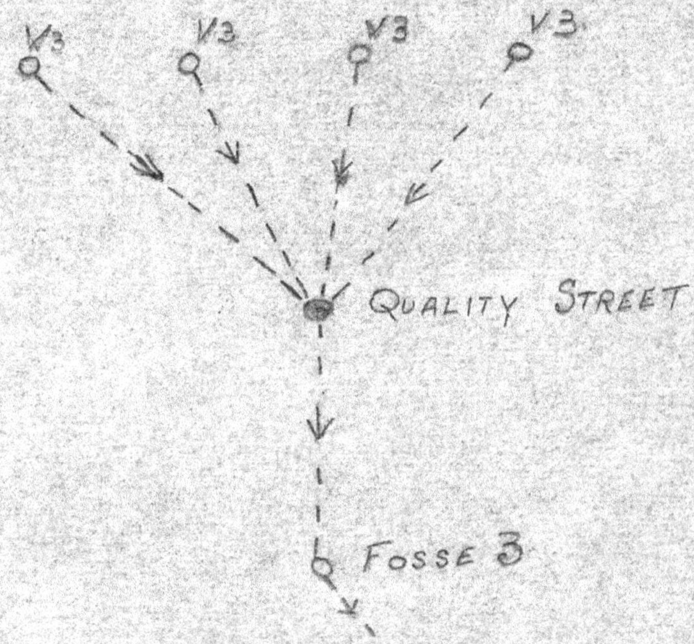

- V3, V3, V3, V3 → Quality Street
- Quality Street → Fosse 3
- Fosse 3 → 15TH DIV HQ

→ Arrow shews direction of Sending

Report of Operations from 21st to 30th September.

Medical Services, 15th Division.

Reference - Map Bethune Combined Sheet 1/40,000.

Regimental Aid Posts.

Those were situated in the trenches as follows:-

44th Infantry Brigade.

1. Near Quality Keep South in communication with Communication trench No.2., which will be kept open for conveyance of wounded only.
(Medical Officers 10th Gordons and 7th Camerons).

2. In the new communication trench No.36. This communication trench will be for wounded only. The dressing station is on the South side of this trench a few yards west of trench "21".
(Medical Officers 9th Black Watch and 8th Seaforths).

46th Infantry Brigade.

1. Just E. of the junction of "21" and new communication trench.
(Medical Officer 10th Scottish Rifles).

2. Close to 1.
(Medical Officer 7th K.O.S.B).

3. In 14.A. Just W. of junction with 9".
(Medical Officer 12th H.L.I.).

4. (a) In "15" just W. of junction with "Northern Up"
   (b) In "14" just W. of junction with "15".
   ((a) and (b) are alternative positions).
(Medical Officer 8th K.O.S.B).

Units R.A.M.C.   The R.A.M.C. units employed were the 45th, 46th and

/47th

47th Field Ambulances, and the 32nd Sanitary Section R.A.M.C. Territorial Force.

Position.	The above units were located as follows:-
48th Field Ambulance.

1. Advanced Dressing Stations

The ABATTOIR, MAZINGARBE.

At the Abattoir, 4 capacious dug-outs were prepared each capable of sheltering 12 lying down cases. Access to two of these was by a door way and steps leading from the interior of the building. These two dug-outs were connected with two others by means of a trench 6 feet broad and about 80 yards long. This was provided with seats on one side for a portion of the way capable of affording accommodation for about 80 sitting cases. A fifth dugout across the road afforded shelter for 12 lying cases.

The Abattoir itself had lying accommodation for 200 cases.

2. REST POST, MAZINGARBE.

At the Brewery, MAZINGARBE and the Chateau next to it.

The above buildings gave housing for 200 lying down and about 200 sitting cases.

3. MAIN DRESSING STATION was located as in the following buildings at NOEUX LES MINES.

(a) Divisional Bath House.
(b) A School House containing 4 large rooms.
(c) A Barn with two large divisions.
(d) The Marie buildings.

The above buildings were able to house 400 lying down cases.

/The

The total accommodation thus provided was therefore:-

	Lying.	Sitting.
1. At Advanced Dressing Station	240	80
2. At Rest Post.	200	200
3. At Main Dressing Station.	400	200
TOTAL =	840	880

46th Field Ambulance.

1. Advanced Dressing Station.

   42 Houses and Cellars at QUALITY STREET.

	Lying.	Sitting.
Accommodation -	350	150

2. Rest Post and Divisional Collecting Station located at Brewery, PHILOSOPHE.

   Capacious cellars were protected from shell fire by sandbags above the roof, and propped up inside with beams to bear the extra weight thus super-imposed. Electric light was laid on.

   Accommodation here provided was for

Lying.	Sitting.
200.	100.

3. Main Dressing Station.

   In converted barns and tents at VAUDRICOURT.

	Lying.	Sitting.
Accommodation =	300.	400.

Total accommodation provided thus was:-

	Lying.	Sitting.
1. Advanced Dressing Station -	350	150
2. Rest Post and Divisional) Collecting Station.)	200	100
3. Main Dressing Station.	300	400
TOTAL =	850	650

47th Field Ambulance.

1. Advanced Dressing Station.

Fosse No.7.

Shelters were provided against the Fosse and protected from shell splinters and shrapnel fire.

	Lying.	Sitting.
Accommodation -	120	120

2. Main Dressing Station.

Located in two school at BOEUX LES MINES.

	Lying.	Sitting.
Accommodation -	400	300

Total accommodation was -

	Lying.	Sitting.
1. Advanced Dressing Station	120	120
2. Main Dressing Station -	400	300
TOTAL =	520	420

The 32nd Sanitary Section.

The Officer Commanding and 9 N.C.O's and men did duty with 47th Field Ambulance and 1 Serjeant and 10 men with 46th Field Ambulance at the Divisional Collecting Station.

All ranks volunteered for this duty which was quite distinct from the service they enlisted for.

Maintenance.   All posts were well lighted and equipped with Medical and Surgical material and food, kitchens and water.

Method of Evacuation.   Special communication trenches were told off for carriage of wounded only from Regimental Aid Posts to the Advanced Dressing Stations at Fosse 7 and QUALITY STREET as follows:-

/1.

1. New Communication Trench No.36.
2. Communication Trench No.2., and
3. Communication Trench No.4 was also available.

A tramway line was constructed running from QUALITY STREET and Fosse 7 to the breweries at PHILOSOPHE and HAZINGARBE. It was for this reason that Rest Posts had to be provided at the termini at these places. The small trucks used at the Colliery were refitted with wooden platforms and rails, and on the platforms 3, and on the rails above 2 lying down cases were carried on stretchers: 25 trollies were provided. These were man handled to and from the breweries.

In addition, 8 wheeled litters were given to each Field Ambulance for use at Advanced Dressing Stations.

From the breweries and Advanced Dressing Station at HAZINGARBE to the main Dressing Stations carriage by motor and horsed ambulances and general service wagons was provided. The 30 cwt motor lorry of the Sanitary Section was fitted with seats capable of holding 24 cases. This plied between the Brewery PHILOSOPHE and the Main Dressing Station of the 46th Field Ambulance at VAUDRICOURT.

Account of the Operations.

The bombardment of the German position began on the 21st September. On the night previous thereto, the Advanced Dressing Stations at Fosse 7 and QUALITY STREET were opened, a bearer subdivision of the 47th Field Ambulance being sent to the former and a similar detachment of the 46th Field Ambulance to the latter place.

/At

At PHILOSOPHE Brewery the 46th Field Ambulance had a tent subdivision: at MAZINGARBE, the Rest Post was occupied by 1 officer and 7 other ranks, and the Advanced Dressing Station at the Abattoir by 2 bearer subdivisions, of the 46th Field Ambulance.

The main dressing stations of the 47th Field Ambulance at NOEUX LES MINES and the 46th Field Ambulance at VAUDRICOURT were open also on the evening of 20th September. The 45th Field Ambulance opened its Main Dressing Station at NOEUX LES MINES on 24th September.

Up to the morning of September 25th, the daily casualty list of wounded was as follows:-

    21st September   1
    22nd September   9
    23rd September   11
    24th September   19
    25th September to 6 a.m.   26

         TOTAL = 66

On the evening of September 24th the strength of the Advanced Dressing Stations was increased as follows:-

Fosse 7 by 2 bearer subdivisions of 47th Field Ambulance.

QUALITY STREET by 2 bearer subdivisions of 46th Field Ambulance.

Divisional Collecting Station by 1 N.C.O. and 10 men of the 32nd Sanitary Section R.A.M.C., Territorial Force.

On the morning of 25th September the Infantry assault was preceded at 5.50 a.m. by a gas and smoke attack: at 6.30 a.m. the Infantry stormed the enemy's trenches with the bayonet and casualties very shortly began to arrive at the Advanced Dressing Stations. The process of clearing the field worked well: as the troops advanced the Regimental Medical Establishments followed up forming new Aid Posts in more advanced positions, contact was well maintained between these

/Regimental

Regimental Stretcher Bearers and those of the bearer divisions of the 46th and 47th Field Ambulances; the wounded unable to walk were conveyed by stretcher carriage to the Advanced Dressing Stations at Fosse 7 and QUALITY STREET. The tramway from the Advanced Dressing Stations worked to the Divisional Collecting Station at PHILOSOPHE, and by this means the wounded were rapidly evacuated, those ~~were~~ able to walk followed in most cases the branch of the tramway to MAZINGARBE and were admitted to the Rest Post and Advanced Dressing Station of the 45th Field Ambulance at this place.

From PHILOSOPHE Brewery evacuation was by the 21 Motor Ambulance Vehicles of the Divisional Field Ambulances, and the Sanitary Section Motor Lorry, to the Main Dressing Stations of the 45th and 47th Field Ambulances at NOEUX LES MINES, and of the 44th Field Ambulance at VAUDRICOURT.

The Motor Ambulance vehicles also cleared on Saturday QUALITY STREET and Fosse 7 by day, but on Sunday, owing to heavy shell fire they were driven back and were unable to clear from there until the evening.

The horse ambulance wagons and general service wagons cleared from the Divisional Collecting Station and Stations at MAZINGARBE to all the Main Dressing Stations.

On Saturday afternoon 25th September, I sent on a bearer subdivision of the 44th Field Ambulance under Lieut. J.R. Turner R.A.M.C. to LOOS to endeavour to bring in wounded from there. He went forward collecting them, but his party was subjected to shell fire and was also gassed by asphyxiating shells. This officer was subsequently wounded and admitted to a Field Ambulance.

On Sunday 26th September I ordered "Q" Section 45th Field

/Ambulance

Ambulance to proceed to LOOS and there open a Dressing
Station. The section opened one in a house at G.34.d.6.9.
on the LOOS Road and collected wounded until Monday at noon
27th September when they were shelled out of it. The
officer i/c , Captain H.R.Friedlander, R.A.M.C., was badly
gassed but had all his wounded removed by stretcher carriage
to QUALITY STREET. He remained behind and endeavoured under
heavy shell fire to put his horses in the vehicles and bring
them away. Several horses were killed and others stampeded,
and the equipment was left. He showed very great gallantry
on this occasion.

The casualties in the division during the course of the
operations were enormous. I think I am correct in saying
that they exceeded those on any previous occasion during
the war. The figures speak for themselves. The admissions
were as follows:-

21/9/15 to 6 a.m. 25/9/15	88
6 a.m. to noon 25/9/15.	153
Noon 25/9/15 to noon 26/9/15.	2434
" 26/9/15 " " 27/9/15	1660
" 27/9/15 " " 29/9/15.	448
TOTAL =	4783

Some of the above casualties were amongst men of other
divisions but none the less the work entailed by the Field
Ambulances was the same; the number of these was 889.

The total of casualties of 15th Division reported as
admitted into other divisional Field Ambulances was 403.

The total of the 15th Divisional casualties accounted
for was thus the large number of 4297 of all ranks.

With the exception of about 100 cases all the casualties
admitted to our Field Ambulances, which meant 4600 cases,
had been collected, their wounds dressed, and all ranks fed

/and

and housed by Sunday 26th September at midnight. It was obviously impossible to accommodate such large numbers in the Field Ambulances, so the difficulty was overcome by billeting the lighter cases, which entailed much extra work for the Medical Establishments.

Owing to the blocking of the road by troops the Motor Ambulance Convoy was unable to clear sufficiently to do very much to ease the pressure on the Field Ambulances until the evening of the 27th September. The task therefore of maintaining and redressing the wounded had thus to be continued until Monday 27th September.

The work of clearing the battlefield of wounded had been done so rapidly and well that on the morning of the 27th I was able to place at the disposal of the Director of Medical Services, 1st Army, 14 Motor Ambulances to assist the Motor Ambulance Convoys on the line of communication in evacuating wounded.

Evacuation by No.8 Motor Ambulance Convoy from the 27th September was rapid and by the 29th all cases had been sent to Casualty Clearing Stations except 48 mild gas cases which remained in the 46th Field Ambulance on 30th September. The scheme for removing the wounded worked admirably and it is entirely due to the zeal and devotion to duty of all ranks both of the Regimental Medical and Field Ambulance Establishments that such splendid results were obtained, and the battlefield was cleared of 4800 casualties by Sunday night.

I cannot praise their services too highly; all ranks worked night and day for three days.

In conclusion I should like to place on record the heroism displayed by the wounded which lightened the task of those who had to minister to them. No murmer or groan was heard amongst this assembly of stricken heroes, many

/with

with grevious wounds joking and making light of them and cheering up their wounded comrades.

It was an honour appreciated by all ranks of the Medical Service to serve such men.

In closing this report I wish to place on record the courageous and devoted services rendered to the British Army by Mdlle. Emilienne Moreau, the particulars of which were furnished me by Captain F.A.Bearn R.A.M.C., officer i/c in Medical charge 9th Black Watch. This girl, who is only 17½ years old, was living with another woman in a shop at LOOS in the Church Square. These premises were taken as a Regimental Aid Post by Captain Bearn, and these two women spent the whole of the day and night (25th - 26th September) in helping to carry in the wounded and carry out the dead, also in preparing food and coffee for all, refusing payment. This work was done continuously for 24 hours. When the British troops were making ineffective efforts to dislodge German snipers from the next house, who were firing on the stretcher bearers, this young girl seized a revolver from an officer and went into the back of the house and fired two shots at the snipers. She came back saying "C'est fini" and handed the revolver back to the officer. It is uncertain if the two shots actually killed the men, but the diversion in the rear enabled our men to effect an entrance in front.

Captain Bearn states " I saw many examples of cool courage that day, but none that excelled hers".

(sd) G.T.BEAMISH. Colonel,
A.D.M.S., 15th Division.

WO95/1910 - 3

15 Div HQ Gen Staff & Depts

Aug 1915

15th DIV.
G.S.,
August, 1915

Army Form C. 2118

WAR DIARY
or
INTELLIGENCE SUMMARY
(Erase heading not required.)

Instructions regarding War Diaries and Intelligence Summaries are contained in F.S. Regs., Part II. and the Staff Manual respectively. Title Pages will be prepared in manuscript.

Place	Date	Hour	Summary of Events and Information	Remarks and references to Appendices
GOSNAY	1.8.15	6 a.m.	Relief of 47th Div Arty & R.E. by 15th Div Arty & R.E. completed	
	2.8.15	4 p.m.	Move of Div M.H. Troops to DROUVIN completed	
	2.8.15		8th Pioneers relieved at disposal of 15th Div	
		6 a.m.	10th Londons relieved at disposal of G.O.C. 4th Inf Bde	
	3.8.15	1 a.m.	Relief of 142 Bde by 44th 2nd Inf Bde completed	
DROUVIN	3.8.15	12 noon	Hd Qrs opened at DROUVIN.	
	3.8.15	4.30 p.m.	Relief of 141st 2 Bde by 46th 2nd Bde completed.	
	4.8.15	1.30 a.m.	Relief of 140th Bde by 45th Bde completed	
		6 a.m.	The 1st Div assumed command over all troops defending the line from the GRENAY-CITÉ JEANNE D'ARC road about 250 yards S.E. of GRENAY Church to the road from LE BUTOIRE to LOOS. This position was divided into 2 sections W and X each held by one brigade, the right or W section was subdivided into 3 subsections each held by 1 Battn with 1 Battn in reserve in NORTH MAROC. The left or X section was divided into 2 subsections each held by 1 Battn with 1 Battn with 1 Battn in reserve at "QUALITY STREET" a collection of horses about 2000 yds S.E of the HALTE de VERMELLES and 1 Battn in reserve at the HALTE de VERMELLES known as PHILOSOPHE	

WAR DIARY or INTELLIGENCE SUMMARY

Army Form C. 2118

Place	Date	Hour	Summary of Events and Information	Remarks and references to Appendices
DROUVIN	4.8.15		The right or W sector was generally about 400 to 500 yds from the enemy trenches. The left sector was within about 20 yds for a distance of about 120 yds. The rest of the front was very good from 200 yds to 600 yds. The whole of the enemy front trenches could be seen from the right sector but on the left they were partly hidden by a fold of the ground. The front was generally quiet except for some shelling of WINCK. There was some sniping & artillery fire, otherwise quiet. Reconnaissance were made of work required to be done & complete organization of defences.	
	5.8.15			
	11.8.15	1.30 pm	46th Inf Bde relieved 44th Inf Bde in Sector W. The reserve brigade moved to NUEUX LES MINES & MAZINGARBE. The reserve Battn in Sector W was billeted in LES BREBIS instead of in N.MAROC	
	12.8.15		A divisional bombing school was started at NUEUX LES MINES & the first course being for instructors.	
	19.8.15	1.45 pm	44th Inf Bde relieved 45th Inf Bde in Sector X. The reserve battns of the 44th Bde were billeted at the HALTE de VERMELLES and at MAZINGARBE instead of at PHILOSOPHE and at the HALTE de VERMELLES. PHILOSOPHE being abandoned owing to its having been frequently shelled.	

Army Form C. 2118

WAR DIARY
or
INTELLIGENCE SUMMARY
(Erase heading not required.)

Place	Date	Hour	Summary of Events and Information	Remarks and references to Appendices
DROUVIN.	26th	12.15am	Two Battns 46th Bde in Sector W relieved by 2 Battns 140th Bde 47th Div	
	27th	1 am	Two battns 46th Bde in Sector W relieved by 2 Battns 140th Bde 47th Div.	
		6 am.	The front of the division consisted now of Sector X only, though the artillery of the Div was covering the front of Sector W in addition to Sector X. The 46th Bde on relief moved to the area FOUQUEREUIL – LA BEUVRIERE – BUSNAY.	

Chateau DROUVIN
31-7-15-

Maxwell Stuart
Lt Colonel. G.S.
15th Division

www.ingramcontent.com/pod-product-compliance
Lightning Source LLC
Chambersburg PA
CBHW081435160426
43193CB00013B/2292